VISION 2000

Praying Scripture
in a Contemporary Way

Mark Link, S.J.

A
Cycle

TABOR
PUBLISHING

Allen, Texas

IMPRIMI POTEST
Bradley M. Schaeffer, S.J.

NIHIL OBSTAT
Rev. Robert Coerver
Censor Liborum

IMPRIMATUR
† Most Rev. Charles V. Grahmann
Bishop of Dallas

December 23, 1991

The *Nihil Obstat* and *Imprimatur* are official declarations
that the work contains nothing contrary to Faith and
Morals. It is not implied thereby that those granting the
Nihil Obstat and *Imprimatur* agree with the contents,
statements, or opinions expressed.

ACKNOWLEDGMENT

Unless otherwise noted, all Scripture quotations are
from the *Good News Bible*, in Today's English Version.
Copyright © American Bible Society 1966, 1971, 1976.
Used by permission.

Send all inquiries to:
Tabor Publishing
200 East Bethany Drive
Allen, Texas 75002-3804

ISBN 0-7829-0103-4
    4 5 6 7   97 96 95 94

VISION 2000

is a daily
meditation program.

This first book of the program
is based on the common *Lectionary*
readings for —

Sunday: Gospel (A Cycle)
Weekday: Gospel

CONTENTS

CONTENTS

About *Vision 2000*

Lance Morrow opened *Time* magazine's cover story "Man of the Decade" (January 1990) with these memorable words:

"The 1980s came to an end in what seemed like a magic act, performed on a world-historical stage. Trapdoors flew open, and whole regimes vanished. The shell of an old world cracked, its black iron fragments dropping away, and something new, alive, exploded into the air in a flurry of white wings."

Morrow was referring to the collapse of the Berlin wall and Communism in Eastern Europe. What nobody dreamed could happen in our century happened in months.

This history-making event recalls Jesus' words to the people of his day:

"When you see
a cloud coming up in the west,
at once you say that
it is going to rain—and it does.
And when you feel the south wind blowing,
you say that
it is going to get hot—and it does. . . .
You can look at the earth and the sky
and predict the weather;
why, then, don't you know
the meaning of this present time?"

LUKE 12:54-56

Vision 2000 was inspired by the conviction that the fall of the Berlin wall and Communism has a special "meaning" for "this present time." If this history-making event could happen against all odds, with such rapidity, is it not a "sign" that other walls can fall as well:

- walls of prejudice,
- walls of injustice,
- walls of exploitation,
- walls of hatred,
- walls of hunger?

Vision 2000 is an invitation to all Christians to join together in prayer for an outpouring of the Holy Spirit upon the human race as it prepares to cross the threshold into a new century. It is an invitation to pray that the new century will see the beginning of a new fall of the "walls" that divide our human family.

How to Use *Vision 2000*

Vision 2000 is based on the common *Lectionary* readings used jointly by Catholics and many Protestants. In other words, the Scripture readings in *Vision 2000* follow the Sunday and daily readings used in worship by many Christians.

There are two ways to pray *Vision 2000:*

• on your own or
• as a member of a support group.

If you pray it *on your own,* simply spend ten minutes a day reflecting on the daily Bible reading.

If you pray it *as a member of a support group* (seven or eight people), spend ten minutes a day reflecting, by yourself, on the daily Bible reading; then meet regularly (ideally, once a week) with the support group.

The purpose of the small-group meetings is twofold:

• to *support* one another in the commitment to daily reflection, and
• to *share* with one another insights, ideas, or thoughts gleaned from the daily reflections.

Daily Reflection Format

Each reflection exercise contains the same four elements:

- a Scripture passage, taken from the common *Lectionary* readings;
- a story from daily life that relates to the passage;
- an application of the passage and the story to your personal life;
- a thought that relates to the passage, the story, and your life.

The format for praying each daily reflection involves three steps:

- reflection preparation,
- reflection proper,
- reflection conclusion.

Reflection Preparation

Begin each reflection by putting yourself in God's presence (a key to serious prayer). One way to do this is to pray this prayer slowly and reverently:

> Father, you created me
> and put me on earth for a purpose.
> Jesus, you died for me
> and called me to complete your work.
> Holy Spirit, you help me
> to carry out the work
> for which I was created and called.

In your presence and name—
Father, Son, and Spirit—
I begin my reflection.
May all my thoughts and inspirations
have their origin in you
and be directed to your glory.

Reflection Proper

The format for each reflection involves the
following:

- *Read* the reflection exercise slowly. When
  you finish, return to any phrase, sentence,
  or idea that struck you while reading.
  (Spend about one minute on this step.)
- *Think* about the phrase, sentence, or idea
  that struck you. Might it be addressing
  something in your life?
  (Spend about four minutes on this step.)
- *Speak* to God about your thoughts. Talk to
  God as you would to a close and trusted
  friend.
  (Spend about one minute on this step.)
- *Listen* to God's response. How might God
  answer you? Don't force this part of your
  reflection. Simply rest in God's presence
  with an open mind and heart. You might
  wish to begin by saying with Samuel:
  "Speak, LORD, your servant is listening"
  (1 Samuel 3:9).
  (Spend about four minutes on this step.)

N.B.: God often speaks to us outside the time of prayer. (Listening for God's response begins in prayer and continues subconsciously throughout the day.)

Reflection Conclusion

End each reflection by praying the Lord's Prayer slowly and reflectively.

After you have concluded the Lord's Prayer, rest momentarily in God's presence. When you feel ready, review your reflection briefly. Then, jot down in a small notebook some "fruit" (idea, thought, or inspiration) from your reflection. This practice is *doubly* helpful if you are in a support group. It makes sharing with the other members easier and more profitable.

N.B.: For handy reference, a summary of the "Daily Reflection Format" is printed on the inside front cover of this book.

Weekly Meeting Format

The purpose of the weekly meeting is for
support and *sharing*. Its success will depend
on two things:

* the *interaction* of the group and
* the *inspiration* of the Holy Spirit.

There is no gimmick to insure success. The
meeting consists in sharing the thoughts that
came to the members in their daily reflections.

The agenda for each weekly meeting involves
three simple steps:

* starting the meeting,
* conducting the meeting, and
* ending the meeting.

Starting the Meeting

The leader calls each meeting to order promptly
at the designated time. (Meetings are thirty to
forty minutes long, unless the group decides
otherwise.) The meeting starts with the
following "Call to Prayer":

A member lights a candle on the table around
which the group is gathered. A second member
then reads aloud the following Bible passage
(John 8:12) and prayer:

[Jesus said,]
"I am the light of the world. . . .
Whoever follows me
will have the light of life
and will never walk in darkness."

Lord Jesus, you said
that where two or three
come together in your name,
you are there with them.
The light of this candle
symbolizes your presence among us.
And, Lord Jesus,
where you are, there, too,
are the Father and the Spirit.
And so we begin our meeting
in the presence and the name
of the Father, the Son,
and the Holy Spirit.

Conducting the Meeting

The meeting proper begins with the leader
responding briefly (two minutes) to these two
questions:

- How faithful was I to my commitment to
  reflect daily on the Bible reading? (This
  question may be omitted after the members
  get in the habit of prayer.)
- Which Bible reading and reflection did I find
  especially rewarding—and why?

The leader then invites each member, in turn, to respond briefly (two minutes per person) to the same two questions.

When all have responded, the leader opens the floor to anyone who wishes—

- to elaborate on his or her response to the second question or
- to comment on another's response (but not to take issue with it or to offer advice). For example, a member might say to another member, "I really was moved by what you shared. Could you elaborate on it a bit more?"

An important point is in order here. The group should be patient with the sharing process. It may take a little time for the group to develop this process—depending on how well the members know, trust, and bond with one another. Some members may be a bit shy, at first, to "share their faith" with others. They will have to be gentle with themselves and one another on this point. Members will find that when they begin to share, the experience is both enriching and affirming.

One final point needs stressing. The purpose of the meeting is not to "discuss" topics but to "share" faith.

Ending the Meeting

The leader ends the meeting promptly at the designated time. (If some members wish to continue, they should do so after the meeting.)

The meeting concludes with a "Call to Mission": a call to witness to Jesus and his teaching. It consists in having a member of the group read the following prayerfully:

> We conclude our meeting
> by listening to Jesus say to us
> what he said to his disciples
> in his Sermon on the Mount:

> *"You are like light for the whole world.*
> *A city built on a hill cannot be hid.*
> *No one lights a lamp*
> *and puts it under a bowl;*
> *instead he puts it on a lampstand,*
> *where it gives light*
> *for everyone in the house.*
> *In the same way*
> *your light must shine before people,*
> *so that they will see*
> *the good things you do*
> *and praise your Father in heaven."*
>
> MATTHEW 5:14-16

Then a member extinguishes the candle (lit at the start of the meeting). The reader concludes:

The light of this candle
is now extinguished.
But the light of Christ in each of us
must continue to shine in our lives.
Toward this end we pray together
the Lord's Prayer: "Our Father . . ."

N.B.: For handy reference, a summary of the "Weekly Meeting Format" (with the readings and prayers to be used) is printed on the last page and inside back cover of this book.

One Final Point

The *Lectionary* readings vary from year to year, depending on what date Easter falls. This leads to complications in some instances. For simplicity's sake, therefore, brief sections of *Vision 2000* are adapted. Likewise, for simplicity's sake, special *Lectionary* readings for special days are omitted.

Finally, the *Lectionary* readings in this volume are based on—

• the Sunday readings: A Cycle (Gospel) and
• the weekday readings: Gospel.

SEASON
OF
ADVENT

[Jesus said,]
"If the owner of a house knew the time
when the thief would come . . .
he would stay awake. . . .
So then, you also must always be ready,
because the Son of Man will come . . .
when you are not expecting him."

MATTHEW 24:43-44

One day, while filing away papers,
the secretary of President J. F. Kennedy
found this note,
written in the president's own hand.
It read:
"I know there is a God—
and I see a storm coming.
If he has a place for me,
I believe that I am ready."

Jesus' warning to be ready
and Kennedy's readiness to serve
invite me to ask:
How ready am I
to put myself at God's service
for whatever God may ask me to do?

I heard the Lord say,
"Whom shall I send?" . . .
I answered,
"I will go! Send me!"

ISAIAH 6:8

MONDAY
Advent
Week 1 _____

[A Roman officer said to Jesus,]
"Sir, my servant is sick in bed at home,
unable to move and suffering terribly."
"I will go
and make him well," Jesus said.
"Oh no, sir," answered the officer.
"I do not deserve to have you come
into my house. Just give the order,
and my servant will get well."

MATTHEW 8:6–8

Bell Telephone executive Birch Foracker
had a deep concern for his workers.
One night he left a dinner group
standing in formal attire on the street
while he climbed down into a manhole
to let a crew of workmen know
that he appreciated their working late.

The stories of the Roman officer and
of Birch Foracker invite me to ask:
What is one way that I can begin
to relate more appreciatively
to those with whom I work and live?

None goes his way alone.
All that we send into the lives
of others,
Comes back into our own.

EDWIN MARKHAM

[Jesus said to his disciples,]
"How fortunate you are
to see the things you see!
I tell you that many prophets and kings
wanted to see what you see,
but they could not, and to hear
what you hear, but they did not."

LUKE 10:23-24

Dutch painter Vincent van Gogh
produced more than 1,700 paintings
and drawings in his lifetime.
He sold only one of them—for $85.
Van Gogh died thinking he was a failure.
Yet, a century later, his painting
Dr. Gachet sold for $82.5 million.

Van Gogh never saw in his lifetime
what he hoped to see.
He never heard what he hoped to hear.
Yet, like the prophets and kings of old,
he stayed the course.
Van Gogh's example prompts me to ask:
What is my chief motivation
in staying the course I am pursuing?

The only ones among you
who will be really happy
are those who have sought and found
a way to serve. ALBERT SCHWEITZER

WEDNESDAY
Advent
Week 1 _____

[One day Jesus asked his disciples
for their few loaves and fish
to feed a hungry crowd of people.
Jesus took them,] gave thanks to God,
broke them, and gave them . . . .
to the people.
They all ate and had enough.

MATTHEW 15:36-37

Mother Teresa
felt called by Jesus to help the poor,
especially those in India's slums.
She began by using all the money she had
to buy a small dirt-floor shack.
Today that shack has multiplied itself
into 100 schools for children
and 150 homes for dying people.

Mother Teresa
gave her "loaves and fish" to Jesus,
and he multiplied them
beyond her wildest dreams.
What "loaves and fish" might I give
to Jesus to be multiplied by him?

Yours are the only hands
with which he can do his work. . . .
Yours are the only eyes
through which his compassion
can shine upon a troubled world.

SAINT TERESA OF AVILA

[Jesus said,]
"Not everyone who calls me 'Lord, Lord'
will enter the Kingdom of heaven,
but only those who do what
my Father in heaven wants them to do."

MATTHEW 7:21

G. Gordon Liddy, White House aide,
was convicted in the Watergate scandal
that forced President Nixon to resign.
After his release from prison,
Liddy underwent a religious conversion.
"The hardest thing I do now," he says,
"is to pray, 'What does Jesus want,
not what does Gordon want?'"

Liddy's prayer invites me to ask, too:
What does Jesus—not I—want?
It also invites me to ask:
How does Jesus reveal to people like me
what he wants them to do?

[An all-pro football star writes:]
I often wonder
where my life is heading,
and what is my purpose here on earth
besides playing the silly games
I play every Sunday.
I feel there's got to be
more to life than that.

JERRY KRAMER, *Instant Replay*

FRIDAY
Advent
Week 1 _____

[Two blind men called out to Jesus,]
"Have mercy on us, Son of David!" . . .
[Jesus] asked them,
"Do you believe that I can heal you?"
"Yes, sir!" they answered.
Then Jesus touched their eyes and said,
"Let it happen . . ."
and their sight was restored.

MATTHEW 9:27-30

A *Peanuts* cartoon shows Charlie Brown
standing in front of his home.
He shouts to passersby, "Believe in me!"
But they pay no attention to him.
Finally, Charlie sighs and says sadly,
"I can't get people to believe in me."

Jesus had the same problem.
Many people refused to believe in him.
Those who did believe, however,
experienced miracles in their lives.
What is one thing that keeps my faith
in Jesus from being stronger than it is?

[Jesus said,] "If you had faith
as big as a mustard seed,
you could say to this mulberry tree,
'Pull yourself up by the roots
and plant yourself in the sea!'
and it would obey you."

LUKE 17:6

As [Jesus] saw the crowds,
his heart was filled with pity . . .
because they were worried and helpless,
like sheep without a shepherd.
So he said to his disciples,
"The harvest is large,
but there are few workers to gather it in."

MATTHEW 9:36-37

Saint Katherine Drexel came from
a wealthy Philadelphia family.
One day, while visiting the city's slums,
she was filled with pity
at the sight of the children living there.
Seeing such a "large harvest"
and so "few workers to gather it in,"
she decided to found
an order of religious women
to help these children.

What is one thing in today's world
that fills me with pity?
What is one thing I might do to help
address this problem in a concrete way?

What does love look like?
It has feet to go to the poor and needy.
It has eyes to see misery and want.
It has ears to hear
the sighs and sorrows of others.

SAINT AUGUSTINE

SUNDAY
Advent
Week 2 _____

[John the Baptist began preaching,]
"Turn away from your sins . . .
because the Kingdom of heaven is near!"

MATTHEW 3:2

Years ago, a man was shocked
to read his own obituary
in the morning paper.
His death was mistakenly reported.
But what shocked him most
was how the obituary described him:
as someone who had devoted his life
to making weapons of war.
That morning he resolved
to turn his energies in a new direction:
working for world peace
and human betterment.
That man was Alfred Nobel,
founder of the Nobel Peace Prize.

John the Baptist's warning to us
to turn from our sins and Nobel's decision
to turn his energies in a new direction
challenge me to inventory and reassess
my own goals in life.

[Jesus said,]
"Will a person gain anything
if he wins the whole world
but is himself lost or defeated?"

LUKE 9:25

[Some people
brought a paralyzed man to Jesus
to be healed.]
When Jesus saw how much faith
they had, he said to the man,
"Your sins are forgiven." . . .
At once the man got up.

LUKE 5:20, 25

Cardinal Bernadin observes
that before we can follow Jesus,
we must experience conversion.
We must come to know and love him.
One way to get to know Jesus
is to open myself more fully to him
in regular, daily prayer.

Cardinal Bernadin's observation
and Jesus' healing of the man
invite me to look into my heart
and ask this question:
What is one thing that keeps me
from opening myself
more fully to Jesus in prayer?

The LORD said, "I was ready
to answer my people's prayers,
but they did not pray.
I was ready for them to find me,
but they did not even try."

ISAIAH 65:1

TUESDAY
Advent
Week 2 _____

[Jesus said,] "What do you think a man does
who has one hundred sheep
and one of them gets lost?
He will leave the other ninety-nine . . .
and go and look for the lost sheep.
When he finds it, I tell you,
he feels far happier over this one sheep
than over the ninety-nine
that did not get lost.
In just the same way your Father in heaven
does not want any of these little ones
to be lost."   MATTHEW 18:12-14

A mother was informed that
her partially deaf son was unteachable.
She responded, "I'll teach him myself."
That son was Thomas Edison,
the inventor of the electric light.

Mrs. Edison's story invites me to ask:
Is there anything I can do
to help implement the Father's plan
so that not "any of these little ones"
shall ever be lost?

I believe that each newborn child
arrives on earth with a message
to deliver to mankind . . .
[and] must be treated as top-sacred.
                                    SAM LEVINSON

WEDNESDAY
Advent
Week 2

[Jesus said,] "Come to me, all of you
who are tired from carrying heavy loads,
and I will give you rest.
Take my yoke and put it on you,
and learn from me, because I am gentle
and humble in spirit."

MATTHEW 11:28-29

Thomas Merton's writings
still impact the thinking of our world.
One day, while he was sitting outside,
a moth settled on his hand.
He writes:
"It would not go away, until,
needing my hand, I blew it lightly
[and it fluttered off into the woods]."
There's something beautifully gentle
about that image.
It's something Jesus might have done.

The gentleness of Jesus
inspires me to inventory my own life:
How gentle am I in dealing with people
and with the things of nature?

The LORD says . . .
"I have filled [my servant]
with my spirit. . . .
He will not break off a bent reed
nor put out a flickering lamp."

ISAIAH 42:1, 3

THURSDAY
Advent
Week 2 _____

*[Jesus said,] "John the Baptist
is greater than any man who has ever lived.
But he who is least
in the Kingdom of heaven
is greater than John."* MATTHEW 11:11

Microphones make the softest voice
louder than the world's loudest voice.
Cars make the slowest person
faster than the world's fastest runner.
Likewise, belonging to God's Kingdom
makes the least person
greater than John the Baptist.
But membership in God's Kingdom
carries with it the responsibility
to work for the completion
of God's Kingdom on earth—
to root out what needs to be rooted out
and to plant what needs to be planted.

In the immediate world in which I live,
what is one concrete thing that needs
to be rooted out? Planted? How to do it?

*[After I die,] I want it said of me
that I plucked a weed
and planted a flower
wherever I thought
a flower would grow.*

ABRAHAM LINCOLN

[Jesus said,] "When John came,
he fasted and drank no wine,
and everyone said, 'He has a demon in him!'
When the Son of Man came,
he ate and drank,
and everyone said, 'Look at this man!
He is a glutton and wine-drinker.' "

MATTHEW 11:18-19

A *Peanuts* cartoon shows Lucy
looking up at the sky and saying,
"Sometimes clouds form actual words."
Charlie Brown says,
"They're not clouds; that's skywriting."
Unmoved, Lucy says, "As I was saying,
sometimes clouds form actual words."

Lucy's reaction to Charlie—
like people's reaction to John and Jesus—
dramatizes a sad fact:
when we close our minds to truth,
we see things not as they are
but as we are.
This raises a question:
Is there, perhaps, an area in my life
where I might be doing this?

A roomful of geniuses
who have closed their minds to truth
is no better off than a roomful of fools
who are incapable of recognizing truth.

SATURDAY
Advent
Week 2 _____

*[When the disciples of Jesus asked
if Elijah would come before the Messiah,
Jesus said,] "Elijah has already come
and people did not recognize him,
but treated him just as they pleased.
In the same way
they will also mistreat the Son of Man."
Then the disciples understood
that he was talking to them about John.*

MATTHEW 17:12–13

Jesus affirms that it was John
of whom it was said, "He will go ahead
of the Lord, strong and mighty
like the prophet Elijah" (LUKE 1:17).
Jesus also affirms that he himself
will suffer, just as John did.

Jesus' readiness to suffer
to accomplish his Father's will on earth
invites me to explore my own readiness
to suffer to accomplish it.

*Lord, teach me to be generous.
Teach me to serve you as you deserve;
to give and not to count the cost;
to fight and not to heed the wounds;
to toil and not to seek for rest;
to labor and not to ask for reward;
except to know that I am doing your will.*

SAINT IGNATIUS

[Jesus said of John the Baptist,]
"John is the one
of whom the scripture says:
'God said, I will send my messenger
ahead of you to open the way for you.' "

MATTHEW 11:10

The prophet Malachi foretold
that God would send a *forerunner*
"like the prophet Elijah" (LUKE 1:17)
to prepare for the Messiah's coming.
John is that *forerunner.*
His instructions to people are simple:
"Turn away from your sins" (LUKE 3:3).

John's words still apply today.
The first step in preparing
for the coming of Jesus into my life
is to "turn away" from my sins.
If I turn away from them,
Jesus will begin
to enter into my life in a way
that I never dreamed to be possible.

[Jesus said,] *"Listen!*
I stand at the door and knock;
if anyone hears my voice
and opens the door,
I will come into his house
and eat with him.

REVELATION 3:20

SPECIAL NOTE _____

Starting today, the readings in the *Lectionary* vary from year to year. To determine which reflection exercise to use today,

- find the current year,
- read across to the date listed,
- page ahead to that date and begin.

This will put you in the correct sequence from now until Christmas. (For example, if the year is 1995, page ahead to December 18 and begin.)

1992	December 14
1993	December 13
1994	December 12
1995	December 18
1996	December 16
1997	December 15
1998	December 14
1999	December 13
2000	December 18
2001	December 17
2002	December 16
2003	December 15
2004	December 13
2005	December 12
2006	December 18
2007	December 17
2008	December 15
2009	December 14
2010	December 13

DECEMBER 12

_____ Advent

[Some religious leaders asked Jesus,
"Where did you get your right to teach?"
Jesus replied,]
"Where did John's right
to baptize come from:
was it from God or from man?"...
They answered Jesus, "We don't know."

MATTHEW 21:25, 27

The leaders tried to trap Jesus.
But they ended up trapping themselves.
For if they said
that John's right came from *man*,
they would offend those
who accepted John
as God's messenger.
And if they said it came from *God*,
they would condemn themselves,
because they rejected John's baptism.
So they feigned ignorance.

How honest and straightforward am I
with others—and with myself?

This above all:
To thine own self be true;
And it must follow,
as the night the day,
Thou canst not then be false to any man.

WILLIAM SHAKESPEARE, *Hamlet*

DECEMBER 13

Advent _____

[Jesus told a story about a father
who said to his elder son,]
" 'Go and work in the vineyard today.'
'I don't want to,' he answered,
but later he changed his mind and went.
Then the father went to the other son
and said the same thing.
'Yes, sir,' he answered,
but he did not go. . . ."
So Jesus said
to [the religious leaders] . . . ,
"John the Baptist came to you
showing you the right path to take,
and you would not believe him;
but the tax collectors and the prostitutes
believed him."   MATTHEW 21:28-32

How tragic it is to see someone
begin well and end badly!
How inspiring it is to see someone
begin badly and end well!

The story of the two sons
invites me to ask:
Is my relationship with God better now
than it was a year ago?
Five years ago? Ten years ago?

Who stops being better stops being good.
                              OLIVER CROMWELL

DECEMBER 14

_____ Advent

[While languishing in prison,
John the Baptist sent messengers
to ask Jesus if he was the Promised One.
Jesus told the messengers,]
"Tell John what you have seen and heard:
the blind can see, the lame can walk . . .
the deaf can hear. . . .
How happy are those who have no doubts."

LUKE 7:22-23

Why did John send messengers to Jesus?
Had the long hours in prison caused him
to begin to question who Jesus was?
We sometimes forget
that John the Baptist was as human and
as vulnerable to temptation as we are.
In any event, Jesus tells the messengers
to inform John that the signs
that Isaiah foretold about the Messiah
are now happening.

What do I do when my mind is vexed
by faith questions or faith problems?

Through the dark and stormy night
Faith beholds a feeble light
Up the blackness streaking;
Knowing God's own time is best,
In patient hope I rest.
For the full day-breaking!

JOHN GREENLEAF WHITTIER

DECEMBER 15

Advent _____

[Jesus praised the tax collectors.
They] were the ones
who had obeyed God's righteous demands
and had been baptized by John.

LUKE 7:29

Tax collectors
got their jobs by bidding for them.
It was then up to them
to get back their investment—
and make a profit besides.
This system often led to corruption.
One ancient writer
tells of seeing a monument
to an *honest* tax collector.
Such a person was so rare
as to deserve special recognition.
These unsavory tax collectors
were the ones who obeyed the words
of John the Baptist
and were baptized in the Jordan.

On a scale
of one (minimally) to seven (totally),
how open am I to God's grace?
How can I open myself even more?

One does not discover new lands
without consenting
to lose sight of the shore.

ANDRE GIDE

DECEMBER 16

The deeds my Father gave me to do,
these speak on my behalf
and show that the Father has sent me.

JOHN 5:36

Lincoln wrote in his Civil War diary:
"Of all the forms
of charity . . . in the hospitals,
those of some Catholic Sisters
were the most efficient.
More lovely than anything
I have ever seen in art . . .
are the pictures . . .
of those modest sisters going . . .
among the suffering and the dying. . . .
They were veritable angels of mercy."

As the deeds of the Catholic Sisters
said something very special about them,
so the deeds of Jesus
said something very special about him.
This raises a question:
What one thing,
above all others,
do my deeds say about me?

Every tree
is known by the fruit it bears;
you do not pick figs from thorn bushes
or gather grapes from bramble bushes.

LUKE 6:44

DECEMBER 17

Advent _____

This is the list
of the ancestors of Jesus Christ.
[It includes:] Perez and Zerah
(their mother was Tamar) . . .
[and] Boaz (his mother was Rahab).
MATTHEW 1:1-6

Normally, we find only men
in ancient Jewish family trees.
It is unusual, therefore, to find women—
including a prostitute, Rahab—
in Jesus' family tree.
There's something beautiful here.
For on the very first page of the Gospel,
we find a preview of Jesus' ministry.
He will make walls tumble down:
walls between male and female,
Jew and Gentile, saint and sinner.

As Jesus' follower,
I share in his ministry
of making walls tumble down—
walls of discrimination, injustice, etc.
What is one way that I might become
more involved in toppling such walls?

Those who follow in Jesus' footsteps,
who never deviate from his teachings,
find that these teachings
are revolutionary.
CATHERINE DE HUECK DOHERTY

——————————————————— Advent

[Joseph was shocked
when he learned that Mary was pregnant.
But an angel told him in a dream,]
"Do not be afraid
to take Mary to be your wife.
For it is by the Holy Spirit
that she has conceived."   MATTHEW 1:20

A retreat master told some fathers,
"Joseph is a perfect model for you."
One father challenged him, saying,
"Joseph's situation was totally different
from my situation.
He was a saint, his wife was sinless,
and his child was the Son of God.
I'm no saint, my wife is not sinless,
and my child isn't the Son of God."
The retreat master responded,
"Was your wife pregnant before your
marriage and you didn't know by whom?
Did your son leave home for three days
and you didn't know where he was?"

The retreat master's point makes me ask:
What situation, in my life, right now,
invites me to be more trusting?

It is easier for parents to have children
than for children to have parents.
POPE JOHN XXIII (slightly adapted)

DECEMBER 19

Advent _____

[An angel appeared to Zechariah, saying,]
"Your wife Elizabeth will bear you a son.
You are to name him John. . . ."
[Zechariah was confused
and filled with questions, saying,]
"How shall I know if this is so?
I am an old man, and my wife is old also."

LUKE 1:13, 18

Critics ridiculed the Russian novelist
Feodor Dostoevski for reaffirming
his belief in Jesus after a period of
faith-confusion and faith-questioning.
Dostoevski responded to them, saying,
"It is not like a child
that I believe in Christ and confess him.
My hosanna has come forth
from the crucible of doubt."

Did I ever go through a period of
faith-confusion and faith-questioning,
as did Zechariah and Dostoevski?
How do I resolve faith questions now?

I always think the best way to know God
is to love many things.
Love a friend, a wife . . .
whatever you like. . . .
Then, you will know there is a God.
Then, you will believe.

VINCENT VAN GOGH (free translation)

_____ Advent

[An angel appeared to Mary and said,]
"You will become pregnant
and give birth to a son,
and you will name him Jesus. . . ."
"I am the Lord's servant," said Mary;
"may it happen to me as you have said."

LUKE 1:31, 38

Mary's response to God's will—
as revealed to her by the angel—
boils down to this: "Thy will be done!"
It is the most beautiful response
a person can make to God's will.
It is the response
Mary taught her son Jesus to make.
It is the response Jesus taught us
to make in the Our Father.
It is the response Jesus himself made
during his agony in the garden:
"Not my will . . .
but your will be done" (LUKE 22:44).

The responses of Jesus and Mary
to God's will invite me
to evaluate my own response to it.
How readily do I embrace God's will?

What we usually pray to God
is not that his will be done,
but that he approve ours.

HELGA BERGOLD GROSS

DECEMBER 21

Advent _____

Elizabeth
was filled with the Holy Spirit
and said [to Mary] in a loud voice,
"You are the most blessed of all women,
and blessed is the child you will bear!"

LUKE 1:41-42

A shoeshine boy was plying his trade
in New York's Grand Central Station.
A silver medal danced at his neck
as he slapped his shine cloth,
again and again, across a man's shoes.
"Sonny," said the man curiously,
"what's the hardware around your neck?"
"It's a medal of the mother of Jesus,"
the boy replied.
"Why her medal?" said the man.
"She's no different from your mother."
"Could be," said the boy,
"but there's a real big difference
between her son and me."

The boy's devotion to Mary,
the mother of Jesus, invites me to ask:
What role does Mary play in my life?
How might she play an even bigger role?

Hail Mary, . . .
gentle woman, . . . peaceful dove,
teach us wisdom; teach us love.

CAROL LANDRY, "Hail Mary: Gentle Woman"

_____ Advent

Mary said,
"My heart praises the Lord;
my soul is glad because of God my Savior,
for he has remembered me,
his lowly servant!"

LUKE 1:46-48

An anonymous poem reads:
"When you're feeling so important,
And your ego is in bloom,
When you simply take for granted
You're the wisest in the room,
When you feel your very absence
Would leave a great big hole,
Just follow these instructions.
They will humble any soul.
Take a bucket filled with water
Put your hand in to the wrist,
Pull it out, the hole remaining
Is how much you will be missed. . . .
The moral of this story
Is do the best you can.
Be proud, but please remember,"
There's no indispensable man."

To what extent do I believe that unless
I lose myself, I will never find myself?

A mountain shames a molehill
until they both are humbled by the stars.

OLD ADAGE

DECEMBER 23

Advent _____

[John the Baptist's father, Zechariah,
was struck dumb by an angel;
but when John was born,
Zechariah regained his speech.]
Everyone who heard of it
thought about it and asked,
"What is this child going to be?"
For it was plain
that the Lord's power was upon him.

LUKE 1:66

An old schoolteacher
used to bow to her students
before each class.
When asked why she did this, she said,
"Because I don't know
what one of my students might become."
It was this kind of mysterious respect
that people had for John.

The mysterious respect
that people had for John the Baptist
is the kind of respect
that I should have for all young people.
What is one way I might better show
this respect in a concrete way?

Every child comes with
the message that God
is not yet discouraged with us.

RABINDRANATH TAGORE

DECEMBER 24

_____ Advent

[The father of John the Baptist
was filled with the Holy Spirit
and spoke this prophecy:]
"You, my child, will be called
a prophet of the Most High God.
You will go ahead of the Lord
to prepare his road for him."
LUKE 1:76

A technique in TV drama is to present
two or more stories simultaneously,
switching back and forth between them.
That's how Saint Luke presents the stories
of the early lives of John and Jesus.
It's his way of stressing
the close link between John and Jesus.
John is God's "advance person,"
sent to prepare the world for Jesus.
Jesus is God's Son,
sent to save the world from sin.

I am like John the Baptist.
I have been called by God to prepare
the immediate world I live in for Jesus.
What is one way
I might begin to do this better
than I have been doing so far?

I cannot change the whole world,
but I can change a small part of it.
KAY FLORENTINO

SEASON OF CHRISTMAS

DECEMBER 25

_____ Christmas

*The Word became a human being and . . .
lived among us.*　　　　JOHN 1:14

One Christmas day during World War II,
a young family was outside
making a snowman.
Suddenly a plane flew by overhead.
After it had passed, the tiniest child
turned to her father and said,
"Daddy,
how do people climb up to the sky
to get into planes?"
Her father explained that passengers
didn't have to climb up to the sky
to get into the planes.
The planes came down from the sky
to get the passengers.

The child's question
helps to illustrate the mystery
of Christmas.
It celebrates the fact
that I don't have to climb to the sky
to get to God.
God has come down to earth to me.
Where do I meet God easiest on earth?

*It is good to be children sometimes,
and never better than at Christmas.*
CHARLES DICKENS

DECEMBER 26

Christmas Season _____

[Jesus warned his disciples
that they would have to suffer
for their faith, saying,]
"Everyone will hate you because of me.
But whoever holds out to the end
will be saved."   MATTHEW 10:22

TV film directors
sometimes follow a quiet scene
with a noisy, violent scene.
The Church
does this in today's liturgy.
It follows the quiet birth of Jesus
with the violent stoning of Stephen.
This helps to remind us that Christmas
is not only the first day of Jesus' life
but also the first day
of his long, painful journey to Calvary.
It also reminds us that we too
must be ready to suffer for our faith—
as Jesus and Stephen did.

The story of Stephen invites me to ask:
How have I suffered for my faith
in the past? How willing am I
to suffer for it in the future?

Offer yourself
as a living sacrifice to God.
ROMANS 12:1

DECEMBER 27

*[When Mary Magdalene found Jesus' tomb
empty on Easter morning,
she ran to tell] Simon Peter
and the other disciple [John],
whom Jesus loved. . . .
Then Peter and the other disciple
went to the tomb . . . saw and believed.*

JOHN 20:2-3, 8

On several occasions, the Gospel refers
to the apostle John as "the disciple
whom Jesus loved."
John was the son of Zebedee,
a fisherman, and the brother of James.
When Jesus called the two brothers,
they left their nets and followed him.
Jesus nicknamed John and James
the *boanerges,* a Hebrew word meaning
"sons of thunder," or "hotheads."
This suggests that John was a man
charged with emotion and
capable of deep love and commitment.

How deep is my own love of Jesus
and my commitment to him?
What is one way that I might
deepen my love and my commitment?

*Jesus Christ will be Lord of all,
or he will not be Lord at all.*
SAINT AUGUSTINE

DECEMBER 28

Christmas Season _____

[Saint Matthew says that,
in an effort to kill the child Jesus,
Herod] gave orders to kill all the boys
in Bethlehem and its neighborhood
who were two years old and younger.

MATTHEW 2:16

Like James and John,
nicknamed by Jesus "the hotheads,"
Herod was also a person
charged with emotion.
He too was capable of deep love
and commitment.
Unfortunately, Herod's love
turned inward toward himself,
not outward toward others.
As a result,
his life took a course opposite to that
of James and John.
Herod now ranks
among the tragic figures of the Bible.

To what extent
does my own love and commitment
tend to turn inward on myself,
rather than outward toward others?
What is one thing I might do about this?

People who fall in love with themselves,
need have no fear of rivals.

ANONYMOUS

_____ Christmas Season

[Mary and Joseph entered the Temple.
A holy man named Simeon
saw Jesus in Mary's arms.
He went over to Mary.
Then, alluding to Jesus' future suffering,
he said to her,]
"And sorrow, like a sharp sword,
will break your own heart." LUKE 2:35

One day, during World War II,
an American marine patrol on Guam
flushed out and killed
three Japanese soldiers.
Routinely, they searched them
for grenades and intelligence material.
In the pocket of one of the dead men
was a picture of Mary, Jesus' mother.
It was in the pocket
over the Japanese soldier's heart.

Millions of mothers since Mary
have felt swords of sorrow
pierce their hearts,
in the form of war-related violence.
To what extent do I accept war and
the suffering it brings as inevitable?

Mankind must put an end to war
or war will put an end to mankind.
JOHN F. KENNEDY

DECEMBER 30

Christmas Season _____

[An old holy woman named Anna
was worshiping God in the Temple.
When she saw the infant Jesus
in the arms of Mary,
she] gave thanks to God
and spoke about the child
to all who were waiting for God
to set Jerusalem free.   LUKE 2:38

Two women were at a garage sale.
One was looking at some trinkets.
The other came up and asked, "Any luck?"
"No!" said the first, "Just junk!"
She stepped aside for her friend to see.
Almost immediately, her friend spotted
an antique silver crucifix.
It was a rare treasure.

Just as Anna, the old holy woman,
saw through the external poverty
of Mary and Joseph to the inner glory
of the child in Mary's arms,
so the one woman at the garage sale
saw through the "junk" to the "treasure."
To what extent do external things
blind me to the "treasure" in people?

Only when we learn to see the invisible,
will we learn to do the impossible.

FRANK GAINES (slightly adapted)

DECEMBER 31

[John the Baptist] was not the light;
he came to tell about the light . . .
the light that comes into the world
and shines on all mankind.

JOHN 1:8-9

An old Christian poem
concerns the last day of the world.
It describes a cross
appearing in the sky.
From it shines a blood-red light.
The amazing thing about the light
is that it reveals people as they are.
It shines through the stylish suit
of the celebrity and shows
what is in the celebrity's heart.
It shines through the uniform
of the factory worker and shows
what is in the worker's heart.
The point of the poem is
that the light of Christ
reveals all people as they really are.

If my life continues as it is going now,
how comfortable will I be on the last day
standing in Christ's light? Why?

We are really three persons:
the person we think we are,
the person other people think we are,
and the person God knows we are.

JANUARY 1
(Mother of God)
Christmas Season _____

*[The shepherds] found Mary and Joseph
and saw the baby lying in the manger.*
LUKE 2:16

An anonymous college student
composed a poem that reads:
"Today I saw a water lily
growing in a pond,
unconcerned about whether anyone
noticed its astounding beauty.
As I sat there, watching it unfold
its petals noiselessly,
I thought of Mary pregnant with Jesus.
She, too, was unconcerned
about whether anyone
noticed her astounding beauty.
But to those who did,
she shared a secret.
That beauty came not from herself,
but from the Jesus life unfolding
its noiseless petals within her."

The student's poem invites me to ask:
What is one way I might facilitate
the growth of the Jesus life within me
that began when I was baptized?

*Be careful how you live;
you may be the only Bible
some person ever reads.*
W. J. TOMS

JANUARY 2

_____ Christmas Season

*[John the Baptist said,] "Among you stands
the one you do not know. . . .
I am not good enough
even to untie his sandals."*

JOHN 1:26-27

A "puzzle page" in a newspaper
showed a drawing of an outdoor scene.
Beneath it was this question:
"Can you find the girl in the drawing?"
A close examination of the drawing
showed the girl's eyes and eyebrows
concealed in a tree branch.
Another branch hid her mouth and nose.
A cloud revealed her flowing hair.
After you discovered the girl,
that drawing was never the same again.

It is like that with Jesus.
He is in our lives, waiting to be found.
Once we find him,
our lives will never be the same again.
This raises a question: Why might I be
finding it hard to find Jesus in my life?

*One day he will come.
Once in the stillness . . .
you will know . . . not from a book
or the word of someone else,
but through him.*

ROMANO GUARDINI

JANUARY 3

Christmas Season _____

[One day as Jesus was walking by,
John said to those around him,]
"There is the Lamb of God,
who takes away the sin of the world!"

JOHN 1:29

We celebrate the birth of Jesus,
the "Lamb of God," in December.
But some scholars think he was born
in spring during "lambing" season.
They think this because Luke says
that on the night Jesus was born
shepherds had their flocks in the fields.
Normally, flocks were herded into caves
for the night, except in lambing season.
(Crowded caves were bad for lambing.)
This would explain why Joseph and Mary
sought shelter in a cave.
(Caves were empty in lambing season.)
It would be fitting for Jesus to be born
when lambs destined for *sacrifice*
in the Jerusalem Temple were born.
For Jesus himself was destined to be
the *sacrificial* "Lamb of God."

What place does sacrifice (suffering) hold
in my life? How do I react to it?

Jesus came not to eradicate suffering,
but to fill it with his presence.

PAUL CLAUDEL

JANUARY 4

[After Andrew
met and talked at length with Jesus,]
he found his brother Simon and told him,
"We have found the Messiah.". . .
Then he took Simon to Jesus.

JOHN 1:41-42

John's Gospel
mentions Andrew three times.
On each occasion, it describes him
introducing someone to Jesus.
In today's reading, it is Simon Peter.
On another occasion, it is a boy
with five loaves and two fish.
On a final occasion, it is some Greeks.

Andrew's practice
of introducing people to Jesus
invites me to ask myself:
How am I sharing my faith in Jesus
with others—
especially my own family and friends?
What is one way I might do this more
conscientiously than I have been doing?

A reporter asked Mother Teresa,
"What's wrong with the Church today?"
Mother Teresa responded,
"You and I, Sir;
we are what's wrong with the Church,
for we are the Church."

JANUARY 5

Christmas Season _____

[After discovering Jesus,
Philip went to Nathanael and said,]
"We have found the one whom Moses
wrote about in the book of the Law. . . .
He is Jesus . . . from Nazareth."
"Can anything good come from Nazareth?"
Nathanael asked.
"Come and see," answered Philip.

JOHN 1:45-46

Thomas Huxley,
a famous British biologist and an atheist,
asked a man of simple, deep faith,
"What does Jesus mean to you?"
The man hesitated, saying,
"You're a very educated man
and you can dispute anything I say."
But Huxley assured him
that he didn't come to argue.
After the man finished explaining
what Jesus meant to him,
Huxley said, "I'd give my right hand
for your faith in Jesus."

That story makes a good point:
No one can believe in Jesus for us.
We must "come and see" for ourselves.

Faith is like love:
it cannot be forced.
ARTHUR SCHOPENHAUER

JANUARY 6

_____ Christmas Season

*[Some Magi from the East
arrived in Bethlehem,
searching for the newborn king.]
When they saw the child
with his mother Mary,
they knelt down and worshiped him.
They brought out their gifts
of gold, frankincense, and myrrh,
and presented them to him.*

MATTHEW 2:11

Early Christians considered the gifts
of the Magi to be highly symbolic.
Gold is the "king of metals" and is,
therefore, symbolic of Jesus' *kingship*.
Frankincense is used in worship and is,
therefore, symbolic of Jesus' *divinity*.
Lastly, myrrh is used in burials
and is symbolic of Jesus' *humanity*.

If I were to give Jesus one gift
to symbolize the role I'd like him to play
in my life—what might that gift be?
What keeps me from letting Jesus
play that role more fully than he now is?

*Jesus is a path to the lost.
He is a loaf to the spiritually hungry.
He is an arm for the weak.
He is a companion to the lonely.
He is a beacon of hope for all.*

56

SPECIAL NOTE _____

Starting January 7, the *Lectionary* readings vary from year to year. To determine which reflection exercise to use today,

- find the current year,
- read across to the page indicated,
- turn to that page and begin.

This will put you in the correct sequence. (For example, if the year is 1995, turn to page 64, "Week after Epiphany: Saturday" and begin.)

Year	Page
1992	60
1993	62
1994	63
1995	64
1996	167
1997	60
1998	61
1999	62
2000	63
2001	167
2002	59
2003	60
2004	61
2005	63
2006	64
2007	167
2008	59
2009	61
2010	62

SEASON
OF
EPIPHANY

MONDAY

_____ Week after Epiphany

[When the wine ran out at Cana,
Mary said,] "They have no wine."
And Jesus said to her, "Woman,
what concern is that to you and to me? . . ."
His mother said to the servants,
"Do whatever he tells you."
[Jesus had six jars filled with water
and turned the water into wine.]

JOHN 2:3-5 (NRSV)

The word *woman* sounds rude to us.
Actually, it had a far different connotation
in the ancient world.
Odysseus addressed Penelope,
his beloved wife, as "woman."
The Roman emperor addressed
Queen Cleopatra of Egypt by this title.
Perhaps the best way
to think of the word *woman*
is to think of it as the British do
when they address
a "woman of nobility" as *Lady*.

Many Christians turned to Mary for help
in time of need.
This raises a question:
When did I last ask her help? Why then?

Mother of Christ, Star of the Sea,
pray for the wanderer, pray for me.

ANCIENT HYMN

TUESDAY

Week after Epiphany _____

*[As evening fell, the disciples suggested
that Jesus dismiss the people
so that they could go off to find food.
Jesus said,] "You yourselves give them
something to eat."*   MARK 6:37

On Thanksgiving Day of 1985,
175 syndicated cartoonists combined
to give an estimated 90 million readers
this Thanksgiving message:
While most Americans are blessed
with an abundance of food,
450 million people go hungry—
many in our own country.
The overall theme of their message
might be summarized as follows:
Almost as bad as having too little food
is having too much food.
It makes you insensitive to the hungry.

To what extent do I agree
that if a free society cannot help
the many who are poor,
it cannot save the few who are rich?
(JOHN F. KENNEDY)

*They are as sick,
that surfeit with too much,
as they that starve with nothing.*
   WILLIAM SHAKESPEARE, *Merchant of Venice*

WEDNESDAY

_____ Week after Epiphany

[One night some disciples
were caught in a storm on the lake.
Suddenly Jesus appeared walking on the water.
Thinking it was a ghost,
the disciples began to panic.]
Jesus spoke to them at once,
"Courage! It is I. Don't be afraid!"
Then he got into the boat with them,
and the wind died down.   MARK 6:50–51

A little girl was given her own room.
As luck would have it, that very night
a severe thunderstorm struck the area.
"Mommy! Mommy!" she cried.
"Come quick! I'm afraid."
Her mother called back, "Don't worry.
God loves you and is watching over you."
The little girl responded,
"I know that, but right now
I need somebody with skin on."

How aware am I of God's providence
over people—especially the young—
through people like myself?
Can I recall a time when God appeared
to use me to act in another's life?

Help another's boat across, and lo!
thine own has reached the shore.
          OLD HINDU PROVERB

THURSDAY

Week after Epiphany _____

*[One Sabbath Jesus stood up
in the synagogue to read the Scriptures.]
He unrolled the scroll
and found the place where it is written,
"The Spirit of the Lord is upon me,
because he has chosen me
to bring good news to the poor."*

LUKE 4:17-18

An old man in New Guinea
used to spend part of each day
reading the Gospel to illiterate people
in the waiting room of a free clinic.
When his eyesight started to fail badly,
the doctor told him
that he was rapidly going blind.
At once the old man began to memorize
the key sections of the Gospel.
When the old man could no longer read,
he recited the Gospel from memory
to the patients, as they waited
to be treated at the free clinic.

If money were no obstacle,
what would I suggest to bring the Gospel
to people today, especially the poor?

*Evangelism is one beggar
telling another beggar
where he found bread.*

D. T. NILES

_____ Week after Epiphany

[Jesus spent long days healing
and preaching to the people.
At the same time, however,]
he would go away to lonely places,
where he prayed. LUKE 5:16

Among his scientific achievements,
George Washington Carver
produced 300 useful products
from the lowly peanut.
Among these were shampoo and ink.
One day, author James Childers
asked Carver for the secret
behind his achievements.
Carver said that he made it a point
to rise each morning at four o'clock.
Then he said, "I go out into the woods.
There in the early morning stillness,
I listen to God and to his plan for me."
Carver was merely imitating Jesus,
who followed a similar practice
of harmonizing work and prayer.

Since I've begun praying on a daily basis,
how has it affected my everyday work?
My relationship with other people?

One of the greatest necessities in America
is to discover creative solitude.
                                    CARL SANDBURG

SATURDAY

Week after Epiphany _____

*[One day
some disciples of John the Baptist
noted that many other disciples
were leaving him and flocking to Jesus.
John replied, saying of Jesus,]*
*"He must become more important
while I become less important."*

JOHN 3:30

A minister was once very popular.
As he grew older, however,
his health declined—so did his flock.
Then, a dynamic new minister
moved to the same town and
began attracting great crowds.
At this point the old minister said
to his remaining parishioners,
"It's time for us to go there too."
With that, he led his diminished flock
to the new church.
Like John, he saw it was time for him
to decrease and for another to increase.

To what extent do I place the people
I am trying to serve
ahead of my own desires and ambitions?

*People who live solely for themselves
are eventually corrupted
by their own company.*

ANONYMOUS

_____ SPECIAL NOTE

Ordinary Time begins the Sunday following
Saturday, Week after Epiphany. Therefore,
turn to page 167 and begin with Sunday,
Ordinary Time: Week 1.

SEASON
OF
LENT

ASH WEDNESDAY

[Jesus said,]
"When you give something
to a needy person,
do not make a big show of it. . . .
Do it in such a way
that even your closest friend
will not know about it."
MATTHEW 6:2-3

"The Stone Carvers"
won the Academy Award in 1984
for the best documentary film,
short subjects.
It featured a tiny group of artists
who have spent years carving ornaments
for the Washington Cathedral.
Historians tell us that the stone carvers
of the famous medieval cathedrals
never signed their art.
They preferred to work anonymously,
solely for the honor and glory of God.

The story of the stone carvers
and the words of Jesus
about not making a show of what you do
invite me to inventory my motives
for working and giving.

The only things we actually keep
are those we give away.
ANONYMOUS

THURSDAY
Lent
Ash Wednesday Week _____

[Jesus said,]
"If anyone wants to come with me,
he must forget himself,
take up his cross every day, and follow me.
For whoever wants to save his own life
will lose it,
but whoever loses his life for my sake
will save it."   LUKE 9:23-24

Mihajlo Jihajlov
was a Yugoslavian political prisoner.
His book *Underground Notes* says
that when prisoners had to choose
between saving their soul or their body,
those who chose their soul
experienced an infusion of dignity, peace,
and strength.
Those who chose their body
ended up losing both their body and their soul.

Jihajlov's words
invite me to recall a time
when I experienced
an influx of dignity, peace, or strength
after making a soul-wrenching decision.

Wisdom is knowing what to do next.
Skill is knowing how to do it.
Virtue is doing it.

                                    THOMAS JEFFERSON

[Some people asked Jesus,] "Why is it
that we and the Pharisees fast often,
but your disciples don't fast at all?"
Jesus answered, "Do you expect
the guests at a wedding party to be sad
as long as the bridegroom is with them?
Of course not! But the day will come when
the bridegroom will be taken away
from them, and then they will fast."

MATTHEW 9:14-15

One reason why Jews fasted
was to prepare for the coming
of the Messiah and the Kingdom of God.
This explains Jesus' response.
He is saying, in effect: "The Messiah
and the Kingdom have come.
The time for fasting is over.
The time for feasting is here.
To fast now would be like holding open
an umbrella after the rain has stopped
and the sun has begun to shine."

Jesus' response makes me ask myself:
What are some religious acts
that I perform more out of duty
than out of love for God and neighbor?

God doesn't want our deeds;
God wants the love that prompts them.

SAINT TERESA OF AVILA

SATURDAY
Lent
Ash Wednesday Week _____

*[One day Jesus was criticized
for eating with sinners.
He replied,] "People who are well
do not need a doctor,
but only those who are sick.
I have not come
to call respectable people to repent,
but outcasts."* LUKE 5:31-32

In 1984 Velma Barfield was
the first woman in twenty-two years
to be executed in the United States.
In prison, she underwent a conversion.
Evidence of it appears on every page
of her Bible. She once told a friend,
"This Bible is where I get my strength.
I couldn't get up in the morning
much less go through the day
without his Word."

Velma Barfield's remarkable conversion
invites me to reflect on my life:
What area in it cries out most
for conversion and repentance?
How might I begin change in this area?

*Of all human acts,
repentance is the most divine.
The greatest of all faults
is to be conscious of none.*
THOMAS CARLYLE

The Spirit
led Jesus into the desert. . . .
After spending forty days and nights
without food, Jesus was hungry.
Then the Devil came to him and said,
"If you are God's Son,
order these stones to turn into bread."
But Jesus answered, "The scripture says,
'Man cannot live on bread alone,
but needs every word that God speaks.'"

MATTHEW 4:1-4

As a boy, Arturo Toscanini
attended Italy's Royal Academy of Music.
Because he was poor,
he sold to the other students
the meat from his meals
so that he could buy musical scores.

Like Jesus himself,
Toscanini belongs to that elite group
whose generous spirit
has enriched the human race.
His story moves me to recall a time
when I sacrificed to the "hurting point"
for something.
What motivated that sacrifice?

Life must be dedicated to a destiny
in order to have a meaning.
JOSE ORTEGA Y GASSET

MONDAY
Lent
Week 1 _____

*[Jesus said, "At the Last Judgment
the King will say to the righteous,]
'Come, you that are blessed. . . .
I was hungry and you fed me. . . .'
The righteous will then answer . . .
'When, Lord, did we . . . feed you . . . ?'
The King will reply,
'I tell you, whenever you did this
for one of the least important . . . ,
you did it for me!'"*

MATTHEW 25:34–35, 37, 40

When Mike Peters won the Pulitzer prize,
he told a newpaper reporter,
"I couldn't believe it.
I didn't know I was in the running.
It was like someone saying,
'You just won the Boston Marathon.'
And you say, 'I wasn't in that race.'
And they say,
'It doesn't matter; you won anyway.'"

That's how the righteous people felt
in today's gospel.
Their experience prompts me to ask:
What is one thing
I am doing for the Lord's least?

*Tell me whom you love
and I will tell you who you are.*
ARSENE HOUSSAYE

[Jesus said,]
"Your Father already knows
what you need before you ask him.
This, then, is how you should pray:
'Our Father in heaven:
May your holy name be honored;
may your Kingdom come;
may your will be done. . . .' "

MATTHEW 6:8-10

A soldier nearly drowned
when his canoe capsized near a waterfall.
As the water swept him toward death,
the words of the Lord's Prayer
flashed into his mind, and he began to pray.
Suddenly, he experienced
a burst of energy and
a feeling of a presence
that was greater than himself.
He battled the water with new strength
and reached safety just in time.

The soldier's experience makes me ask
about my prayerful contact with God.
When was it strongest in my life?
What keeps it from being stronger now?

Whoever has lost contact with God
lives on the same dead-end street
as the person who denies God.

MILTON A. MARCY

WEDNESDAY
Lent
Week 1 _____

*[Concerning people who sought
a special sign from him, Jesus said,]*
*"In the same way that the prophet Jonah
was a sign for the people of Nineveh,
so the Son of Man will be a sign
for the people of this day."* LUKE 11:30

Jonah was a sign in that his preaching
touched people's hearts,
and they turned away from their sins.
In other words, Jonah's words
had "convincing power"
for people whose hearts were open
(MATTHEW 12:41).
In the same way, Jesus will be a sign
to the people of his time.
For people whose hearts are open,
his words will have "convincing power."

What keeps my heart from being
more open to the words of Jesus?

*[Saint Paul writes,
My message was not] delivered
with skillful words of human wisdom,
but with convincing proof
of the power of God's Spirit.
Your faith, then, does not rest
on human wisdom but on God's power.*
1 CORINTHIANS 2:4-5

[Jesus said,]
"Everyone who asks will receive. . . .
As bad as you are,
you know how to give good things
to your children.
How much more, then,
will your Father in heaven
give good things to those who ask!"

MATTHEW 7:8, 11

A woman kept a list
of special requests she made to God.
She would place them in her Bible
and periodically check them.
She was surprised to discover
how many of them were answered
in ways totally different
from what she expected.
For example, one was answered
by a change of attitude toward a person.

The woman's experience invites me to ask:
When did God answer my prayer
in a way totally different
from what I expected?
How persistent am I in prayer?

The value of persistent prayer
is not that God will hear us,
but that we will finally hear God.

WILLIAM MCGILL

FRIDAY
Lent
Week 1 _____

[Jesus said,] "Whoever is angry
with his brother [or sister]
will be brought to trial. . . .
So if you are about to offer your gift
to God at the altar and there you remember
that your brother [or sister]
has something against you,
leave . . . and make peace . . .
and then come back and offer your gift."

MATTHEW 5:22-24

Just as the traffic light turned green,
the motor of a woman's car died.
When she could not restart it,
the driver behind her began honking.
Again and again she tried—to no avail.
Now, the driver behind her was livid
and began honking irrationally.
Finally, the woman got out of her car,
walked back to the motorist, and said,
"I'll be glad to honk your horn for you
if you'll start my car for me."

The woman's calmness
invites me to ask:
What is one way I might improve upon
my handling of explosive situations?

"Happy are those who work for peace;
God will call them his children!"

MATTHEW 5:9

[Jesus said,]
"You have heard that it was said,
'Love your friends, hate your enemies.'
But now I tell you: love your enemies
and pray for those who persecute you. . . .
Why should God reward you if you love
only the people who love you?"

MATTHEW 5:43-44, 46

Newsweek magazine carried a photo
of three boys kneeling in a church pew.
The story went on to say
that the boys' parents were killed
when a bomb exploded on a plane
over Colorado, killing 41 passengers.
The children of St. Gabriel's—
where the boys attend school—
asked if they could hold
a prayer service for the boys' parents.
The oldest boy said it would be okay.
Then he added, "Could we also pray
for the man who killed my parents?"

Sometimes children put into practice
the difficult teachings of Jesus
far better than adults do. Why?

[Jesus said,] "Unless you change
and become like children,
you will never enter the Kingdom of heaven."

MATTHEW 18:3

SUNDAY
Lent
Week 2 _____

*[Jesus took
Peter, James, and John up a mountain.
Jesus' face became] like the sun. . . .
A shining cloud came over them,
and a voice from the cloud said,
"This is my own dear Son,
with whom I am pleased—listen to him!"*
MATTHEW 17:2, 5

In *Something Beautiful for God*,
Malcolm Muggeridge describes
the impact that Mother Teresa
had upon an audience of people, saying:
"Every face . . . was rapt, hanging on
her words; not because of the words . . .
but because of her. Some quality
came across, over and above the words,
that held their attention.
A luminosity
seemed to fill the school hall . . .
penetrating every mind and heart."

The story of Jesus on the mountain
and the story of Mother Teresa
recall that certain people
have impacted my life deeply.
Who is one of these people?

*Saints are persons who make it easier
for the others to believe in God.*
NATHAN SODERBLUM

[Jesus said,] "Do not judge others,
and God will not judge you."

LUKE 6:37

A young lady was dating a businessman.
The relationship developed
and the man was considering marriage.
To make certain
there was nothing in the woman's past
that would embarrass him, he hired
a detective agency to run a check on her.
The agency assigned an agent
who was not told the client's identity.
When the agent reported back, he said:
"The young lady is a splendid person,
except for one unfortunate blemish.
Lately, she's been dating a businessman
of questionable reputation."

To what extent do I agree
with the statement that "we see things
not as they are, but as we are"?
Who is one person
with whom I live or work
that I may be misjudging?

[Jesus said,]
"Take the log out of your own eye,
and then you will be able to see clearly
to take the speck out of [another's] eye."

LUKE 6:42

TUESDAY
Lent
Week 2 _____

*[Jesus said,] "The greatest one
among you must be your servant.
Whoever makes himself great
will be humbled, and whoever
humbles himself will be made great."*

MATTHEW 23:11-12

Years ago, Miami Dolphins coach,
Don Shula, was vacationing in Maine
with his wife and five children.
One rainy afternoon
they went to the town's only theater.
When they walked in, there were only
six people in the entire theater.
To a person, however,
they stood up and applauded the Shulas.
As Don and his family sat down,
a man ran up and shook Don's hand.
"How did you recognize me?" Don asked.
"Mister," the man said, "I don't know you.
All I know is that just before
your family walked in, the manager said
that unless five more people showed up,
we wouldn't have a movie today."

If Jesus asked my best friend
how humble I am,
how might my best friend answer him?

*Humility isn't thinking little of self;
it isn't thinking of self at all.*

[Jesus said, "If you want to be great,
you] must be the servant of the rest . . .
like the Son of Man,
who did not come to be served,
but to serve and to give his life
to redeem many people."

MATTHEW 20:26, 28

A world statesman was an honored guest
at the coronation of King Edward VII
of England in 1901.
When he returned home, he was asked
what sight impressed him most.
He surprised his questioner, answering:
"I was returning to my hotel one night,
when I saw a boy huddled in a doorway
with his tiny sister.
It was cold,
and the boy had taken off his coat
and wrapped it around her
to keep her warm.
This sight was more impressive
than even the coronation itself."

Why are the very young
often marvelously unselfish?

Life begins as a quest of the child
for the man and ends as a journey
by the man to rediscover the child.

LAURENS VAN DER POST

THURSDAY
Lent
Week 2 _____

*[Jesus told a parable about a rich man
who ignored the plight of a poor man
whom he passed daily outside his gate.
Both died, and their fates were reversed.
The rich man asked Abraham
to send someone back to warn his family,
lest they end up as he did, saying,]*
*"If someone were to rise from death
and go to them,
then they would turn from their sins."*
*But Abraham said,
"If they will not listen to Moses
and the prophets,
they will not be convinced
even if someone were to rise from death."*

LUKE 16:30-31

A rich widow said, "Abraham is saying
that if my dead husband returned, and said,
'Darling, change your life, because
you're making the same mistake I did,'
I'd find some excuse to explain away
his appearance, just to avoid changing."

If a dead friend appeared to me and said,
"Life after death is as Jesus said it is,"
would it make a difference in my life?

*Rabbis used to say
that the rich help the poor in this world
but the poor help the rich in the next.*

FRIDAY
Lent
Week 2

[Jesus told this parable.
"A landowner leased his vineyard
to tenants for a share of the crops.
When harvesttime came, he sent his servants
to obtain his share of the crops,
but the tenants abused and killed them.
A second time the owner sent servants,
but the tenants did the same thing.]
Last of all [the owner] sent his son. . . .
But when the tenants saw the son . . .
they grabbed him . . . and killed him.
[The owner expelled the tenants
and leased the vineyard to new tenants.]"

MATTHEW 21:37-39

This parable summarizes the Bible story.
The vineyard stands for Israel.
The vineyard owner stands for God.
The tenants stand for Israel's leaders.
The servants stand for God's prophets.
The owner's son is Jesus.
The new tenants are Jesus' apostles.

In what way, perhaps, am I like
the original tenants of the vineyard?

All these things happened to [Israel]
as examples for others,
and they were written down
as a warning for us.

1 CORINTHIANS 10:11

SATURDAY
Lent
Week 2 _____

[Jesus told this parable.
"A father had two sons.
The younger one decided to leave.
So, taking his inheritance, he left.
After spending the money foolishly,
he decided to return.]
He was still a long way from home
when his father saw him . . .
and he ran, threw his arms around his son,
and kissed him." LUKE 15:20

A saintly nun told the bishop
that she was having visions of Jesus.
To test her, the bishop said,
"Next time you see Jesus,
ask him what was the bishop's great sin
before he became bishop."
Months later, the sister returned.
The bishop asked,
"Well, what did Jesus say my sin was?"
The sister replied,
"Jesus said he no longer remembered it."

To what extent do I forgive and forget?
How do I usually show other people
that I have forgiven them?

Forgiveness is a funny thing.
It warms the heart and cools the sting.
WILLIAM A. WARD

*[Jesus and a woman
were at a well, talking about water.
After a while, Jesus said to her,]
"Whoever drinks this water
will get thirsty again,
but whoever drinks the water
that I will give . . .
will never be thirsty again."*

JOHN 4:13-14

In *Me and Other Advertising Geniuses,*
Charlie Brower alludes to the folly
of trying to satisfy a spiritual thirst
with a material object.
He says,
"My friend Bill is one of those guys
who's still scoring touchdowns,
even though the game's over and won.
My friend Bill has done everything
they've told him to do,
but he's still thirsty and unhappy."

Do I know anyone like Charlie's friend?
What makes me think this person
is like Charlie's friend?
What might I do to help this person?

*Our hearts were made for you,
O Lord, and they will not rest
until they rest in you.*

SAINT AUGUSTINE

MONDAY
Lent
Week 3 _____

[One day in Nazareth,
some people objected to Jesus' teaching,
because he was only the carpenter's son.
Eventually, the situation got so ugly
that they] dragged Jesus out of town . . .
to throw him over the cliff,
but he walked through the middle
of the crowd and went his way.

LUKE 4:29-30

A mob was about to riot in London.
The chief of police,
who radiated a mysterious strength,
walked slowly toward the angry mob.
When he reached the first row,
the mob fell silent and opened ranks.
He walked right through them, unharmed.
The chief's action was like releasing
the air from a near-bursting balloon.
Jesus radiated a similar
mysterious inner strength in Nazareth.

The story of Jesus and the story
of the chief invite me to recall a time
when I felt the presence of Jesus
radiating powerfully from someone.

Let nothing frighten you. . . .
Who has God, lacks nothing.
God alone is enough.
SAINT TERESA OF AVILA

TUESDAY
Lent
Week 3

Peter came to Jesus and asked,
"Lord, if my brother
keeps on sinning against me,
how many times
do I have to forgive him? Seven times?"
"No, not seven times," answered Jesus,
"but seventy times seven."

MATTHEW 18:21-22

Elizabeth Morris was filled with rage.
A drunk driver, named Tommy,
struck and killed her only son.
Tommy was sentenced to give talks
to students on behalf of MADD
(Mothers Against Drunk Drivers).
One day
Elizabeth went to hear Tommy speak.
Moved by the genuine sorrow and
remorse that he felt for what he did,
she not only forgave him,
but also became his friend.

What might I do if I am finding it hard
to forgive someone who has hurt me?

People who cannot forgive others
break the bridge
over which they must pass
if they are to reach heaven;
For everyone has a need to be forgiven.

GEORGE HERBERT (slightly adapted)

WEDNESDAY
Lent
Week 3 _____

[Jesus said,]
"Whoever disobeys even the least important
of the commandments
and teaches others to do the same,
will be least in the Kingdom of heaven.
On the other hand,
whoever obeys the Law
and teaches others to do the same,
will be great in the Kingdom of heaven."

MATTHEW 5:19

Clara Feldman survived
the Nazi holocaust in World War II.
Today she goes from school to school
to teach students about it, firsthand.
She also tries to apply its lessons
to our modern world.
She warns students,
"We cannot be indifferent to evil.
We cannot shut our eyes to it
and pretend that we do not see it."

Jesus' words and Clara's example
invite us to ask: Is there some evil
that I should protest more vigorously
right now? What might I do?

Who accepts evil
without protesting against it
is really cooperating with it.

MARTIN LUTHER KING, JR.

THURSDAY
Lent
Week 3

[One day Jesus was expelling a demon.]
The crowds were amazed,
but some of the people said,
"It is Beelzebul, the chief of the demons,
who gives him the power to [do this]."

LUKE 11:14-15

The Broadway musical *1776*
dealt with those history-making days
when our ancestors were considering
declaring independence from England.
One night John Adams—a leader
in the fight for independence—was worried.
Well-meaning but misguided citizens
were opposing the declaration.
Standing alone in Independence Hall,
a frustrated John Adams sang:
"Is anyone out there?
Does anyone care?
Does anyone see what I see?"

How do I respond when well-meaning
but misguided people frustrate my efforts
to do what I think is right?
What keeps me moving forward
when this happens?

Patience is power.
With time and patience,
the mulberry leaf becomes silk.
CHINESE PROVERB

FRIDAY
Lent
Week 3 _____

*[Jesus said,] " 'Love the Lord your God
with all your heart, with all your soul,
with all your mind,
and with all your strength. . . .
Love your neighbor as you love yourself.'
There is no other commandment
more important than these two."*

MARK 12:30–31

Ardis Whitman was having difficulty
adjusting to the death of her son.
One night her young granddaughter
and her granddaughter's boyfriend
took her to a nightclub.
When the orchestra played a song
that reminded Ardis of her son,
tears welled up in her eyes.
Spontaneously, the young couple
took her hands into theirs.
That beautiful gesture, said Ardis,
"made God seem very close to me."

The words of Jesus
and the young couple's response to Ardis
make me ask: What one thing might I do
to help bring others closer to God,
especially my own family?

*God does not ask for our ability
or our inability, but our availability.*

ANONYMOUS

[Jesus told a parable
about two people who prayed to God.
He said, "The first prayed,
'God, I thank you that I am not greedy
or dishonest, like other people.'
The second prayed more simply, saying,]
'God, have pity on me, a sinner.'
I tell you," said Jesus,
". . . everyone who makes himself great
will be humbled,
and everyone who humbles himself
will be made great."   LUKE 18:13-14

Cato, an ancient Roman senator,
was walking one day with another senator.
His colleague turned and said,
"Cato, it's a scandal that the senate
has not erected a statue in your honor.
I'm going to look into the matter."
"Please don't," said Cato, "I'd rather
people asked, 'Why isn't there a statue
to Cato?' than 'Why is there one?' "

How concerned am I about receiving
recognition for the things I do?

The more grains of rice on a stem,
the lower it bends.
The fewer grains, the higher it stands.
          MALAYAN PROVERB

SUNDAY
Lent
Week 4 _____

[One day Jesus healed a blind person.
When some Pharisees closed their eyes
to the healing and its meaning,
Jesus said to them,] "I came . . .
so that the blind should see
and those who see should become blind."

JOHN 9:39

Astronaut Ed Aldrin
was involved in the first moon landing.
He said that he hoped
its technical success would not blind us
to its deeper spiritual meaning.
His point was this:
Seen from the moon, our Earth appears
as a tiny spaceship.
That perspective of Earth, says Aldrin,
highlights—for those with eyes to see—
that we are one family under God
and should start living that way.

What tends to keep me from seeing
that we are all one family under God?
How might I keep myself from being
"blinded" by this difficulty?

The Fox said to the Little Prince,
"Now here's my secret:
it is only with the heart
that one can see rightly."

SAINT-EXUPERY, *The Little Prince*

[A Roman official asked Jesus to come
and heal his son.] Jesus said to him,
"Go; your son will live!"
The man believed Jesus' words and went.
On his way home
his servants met him with the news,
"Your boy is going to live!"

JOHN 4:50-51

God told Moses to hold his staff
over the Red Sea, saying that the waters
would part and create a path
for the Israelites to cross to safety.
Legend says the waters didn't part
until the first group of Israelites
actually stepped into the sea.

The faith of the Israelites
and the faith of the Roman official
invite me to ask myself this question:
On a scale of one (not very) to seven (very),
how strong is my faith?
What might I do to strengthen it?

I sought my soul—
but my soul I could not see.
I sought my God—
but my God eluded me.
I sought my brother—
and I found all three.

ANONYMOUS

TUESDAY
Lent
Week 4 _____

[There was a pool in Jerusalem
where people came to be cured.
A man who had been sick
for thirty-eight years was lying there.
Jesus asked him,]
"Do you want to get well?"
The sick man answered,
"Sir, I don't have anyone here
to put me in the pool
when the water is stirred up. . . ."
Jesus said to him,
"Get up, pick up your mat, and walk."
JOHN 5:5-8

Years ago a pair of birds
built their nest on top of a monument
in a main plaza in Buenos Aires.
Three times workmen removed it,
and three times the birds rebuilt it.
Finally, the citizens insisted
that the workmen let the nest stay.

What keeps me from pursuing
my spiritual life as persistently
as I pursue my professional life?

A hammer strikes a rock fifty times,
without a crack appearing.
On the fifty-first blow, the rock splits.
This blow alone didn't split the rock,
but also all those that went before it.

WEDNESDAY
Lent
Week 4

[Jesus said,]
"I am not trying to do what I want,
but only what he who sent me wants."

JOHN 5:30

Hikers and mountain climbers
sometimes experience incredible highs.
A Swiss hiker describes such a high.
Suddenly, she felt
God's power and presence penetrate her.
She was so overwhelmed
that she sat down, saying,
"My eyes overflowed with tears.
I thanked God that . . .
he had taught me to know him.
I begged him ardently
that my life be consecrated to his will."

How ardently do I seek
to know God's will for me?
Why does the idea
of consecrating my life to God's will
attract or frighten me?

God in heaven,
when the idea of you awakes in my heart,
let it not awaken like a frightened bird
that thrashes about in panic,
but like a child waking from a nap—
its face aglow with a trusting smile.

SOREN KIERKEGAARD (free translation)

THURSDAY
Lent
Week 4 _____

[Jesus said,]
"The deeds my Father gave me to do,
these speak on my behalf
and show that the Father has sent me."

JOHN 5:36

Eighty-year-old Clara Hale
has served as foster mother
to over 500 babies
born to drug-addicted mothers.
She cares for them
until their own mothers can do so.
These babies enter life
with a drug dependency themselves.
That makes Mother Hale's job harder.
"When a baby is crying for a drug,"
she says, "all I can do
is hold it close and say to it,
'I love you, and God loves you,
and your mama loves you.
Your mama just needs a little time.'"

Mother Hale's work
testifies to her love for children.
Jesus' work
testifies to his love for his Father.
To what love does my work testify?

Work as though all depends on you.
Pray as though all depends on God.
SAINT IGNATIUS OF LOYOLA

Some of the people of Jerusalem
said [about Jesus], "Isn't this the man
the authorities are trying to kill?
Look! He is talking in public. . . ."
Then they tried to seize him,
but no one laid a hand on him.

JOHN 7:25-26, 30

Joseph Conrad went to sea as a boy.
One day, the captain was teaching him
to steer the ship.
Suddenly a storm blew up.
Instead of taking the wheel from Joseph,
the captain shouted instructions to him:
"Laddie, keep her pointed into the wind!
Laddie, keep her pointed into the wind!"
Jesus followed this same course of action
in his life.
Even though storms raged about him,
he kept himself pointed into the wind.

How do I respond when I meet opposition
to what I think is right?

Far better to dare mighty things . . .
than to take rank
with those poor spirits
who neither enjoy much or suffer much
because they live in the gray twilight
that knows not victory or defeat.

THEODORE ROOSEVELT

SATURDAY
Lent
Week 4 _____

[One day the chief priests and Pharisees
sent an armed guard to arrest Jesus.]
When the guards went back,
the chief priests and Pharisees asked them,
"Why did you not bring him?"
The guards answered, "Nobody
has ever talked the way this man does!"

JOHN 7:45-46

Columnist Sydney Harris wrote:
"My friends are sometimes shocked
when I read a few pages of a new book
and then lay it down with the supreme
conviction that it is not worth reading."
Harris explains that if he (Harris)
began to operate on someone,
a real surgeon could tell at once
that he knew nothing of surgery.
Harris says,
"The same is true of writing."
And it is also true of speaking.
Those who heard Jesus speak
knew at once that he was more than man.

What tells me Jesus is more than man?

Orators spoke to their listeners
of life as it seemed to the mind.
The Nazarene spoke of a longing
that lodged in the heart.

KAHLIL GIBRAN

[When Lazarus died,
Jesus told his sister Martha,]
"Your brother will rise to life."
[Then Jesus added,]
"I am the resurrection and the life.
Whoever believes in me will live,
even though he dies."

JOHN 11:23, 25

Father Walter Ciszek spent 23 years
in Russian prisons and work camps.
Eventually he was released
and returned home to America.
His book *He Leadeth Me* describes
the deep faith in eternal life
that burns brightly in the hearts
of Russia's ordinary people.
All the decades
of atheistic propaganda by the media
have not altered this faith.

What convinces me most
that there is life after death?
What keeps me from living more in accord
with my belief?

If seeds in the black earth
can turn into such beautiful roses,
what might the heart of man become
in its long journey to the stars.

GILBERT K. CHESTERTON

MONDAY
Lent
Week 5 _____

*[Some religious leaders
wanted to stone an adultress.
Jesus said,] "Whichever one of you
has committed no sin
may throw the first stone."* . . .
They all left, one by one. . . .
*[Then Jesus said to the woman,]
"Go, but do not sin again."*

JOHN 8:7, 9, 11

An unknown poet writes:
"How I wish
that there was some wonderful place
Called the Land of Beginning Again,
Where all our mistakes
and all our headaches . . .
Could be dropped
like a shaggy coat at the door,
And never put on again."

There is such a place—in God's heart.
What convinces me most
that God isn't interested in what I was,
but in what I can become?
What was I? What am I becoming?

*Teach me to feel another's woe,
To hide the fault I see;
That mercy I to others show,
That mercy show to me.*

ALEXANDER POPE, "The Universal Prayer"

*[Jesus said,] "When you lift up
the Son of Man, you will know . . .
that I do nothing on my own authority,
but I say only what the Father
has instructed me to say.
And he who sent me is with me;
he has not left me alone,
because I always do what pleases him."*

JOHN 8:28-29

Author Keith Miller got so depressed
that he drove off to a secluded spot.
He started to cry. After a while
he looked up at the sky and said to God:
"Whatever you want from me, take it!"
Suddenly, it occurred to him
that what God wants from us is our will.
That realization changed his life.
He wrote later in *A Taste of New Wine:*
"God wants your will;
and if you give him your will,
he'll begin to show you life
as you've never seen it before."

What keeps me from giving my will over
to God as completely as I would like to?

*With God, go over the sea—
without him,
don't even go over the threshold.*

RUSSIAN PROVERB

WEDNESDAY
Lent
Week 5 _____

*Jesus said to those who believed in him,
"If you obey my teaching,
you are really my disciples;
you will know the truth,
and the truth will set you free."*

JOHN 8:31–32

Charles Colson was a top Nixon aide,
sent to prison in the Watergate scandal.
Later, he experienced a conversion.
He was deeply affected by this passage
from C. S. Lewis's *Mere Christianity:*
"Pride leads to every other vice: it is
the complete anti-God state of mind. . . .
As long as you are proud
you cannot know God. A proud man
is always looking down on things. . . .
As long as you are looking down,
you cannot see something above you."
After reading that passage, Colson said,
"Suddenly I felt naked and unclean. . . .
Lewis's words were describing me."
The truth had set Charles Colson free.

Is there anything in my life that tends
to enslave me, as pride enslaved Colson?

*[Pride] eats up the very possibility
of love, contentment,
or even common sense.*

C. S. LEWIS

THURSDAY
Lent
Week 5

[Jesus said,]
"I am telling you the truth:
whoever obeys my teaching
will never die." JOHN 8:51

Pastor Thomas DeWitt Talmage
had a strong faith in Jesus' promise
that whoever obeys his teaching
would never die.
As a result, he never removed the names
of the deceased parishioners
from the parish registry.
He simply listed them
as having "changed residence."

From a practical point of view,
what is one way
that my faith in eternal life
affects my daily dealings
with other people?
In other words, how is my ordinary way
of relating to other people
and doing business with them
different from that of a good atheist?

What a man believes
may be ascertained, not from his creed,
but from the assumption
on which he habitually acts.
GEORGE BERNARD SHAW

FRIDAY
Lent
Week 5 _____

[When some people tried to stone Jesus,
he asked,] "For which [of my good deeds]
do you want to stone me?"
They answered, "We do not want to stone you
because of any good deeds, but because . . .
you are trying to make yourself God!"

JOHN 10:32-33

Leopold Stokowski was conducting
the Philadelphia Orchestra.
One overture featured a trumpet,
played offstage.
Twice it came time for the trumpet;
twice it failed to sound offstage.
Stokowski was livid.
After the overture he stormed offstage
to find the trumpet player.
There he was—arms pinned to his sides
by a burly security guard who said,
"This nut was trying to play his horn
while your concert was going on."

As the well-meaning guard
frustrated Stokowski's work,
similarly, well-meaning people
frustrated Jesus' work.
How might I, unwittingly, be doing this?

As high as the heavens are above the earth,
so high are my ways and thoughts above yours.

ISAIAH 55:9

*[Jesus healed the people,
taught them, and reached out to them.
He did everything he could to show them
that he loved them. When the leaders saw
this, they met in private, saying,]
"What shall we do? . . .
If we let him go on in this way,
everyone will believe in him."* JOHN 11:47-48

In *My Fair Lady*, Eliza Doolittle
grows weary of Freddy's daily letters
describing his love for her.
In a burst of frustration,
she sings a song called "Show Me."
In it she says she's sick of words—
sick of talk of stars burning above.
"If there's really any love
burning in your heart," she sings,
"show me!"

Jesus had done everything he could
to show his love for the people.
But many rejected his efforts.
Jesus' experience invites me to ask:
How do I respond
when people reject my love for them?

*Love is patient. . . .
Love never gives up. . . . Love is eternal.*
1 CORINTHIANS 13:4, 7-8

SUNDAY
Lent
Week 6 _____

They crucified [Jesus] and then
divided his clothes among them. . . .
Above his head
they put the written notice . . . :
"This is Jesus, the King of the Jews."
MATTHEW 27:35, 37

Some divers discovered a sunken ship.
One of the treasures they found on it
was a man's wedding ring.
Etched on the wide gold band of the ring
was a hand holding a heart.
Under it was this moving inscription:
"I have nothing more to give you."
This inscription
could have been placed on Jesus' cross.
For by his death,
Jesus gave us everything he had:
his body, his blood, his love, his life.
He had nothing more to give us.

To what extent have I given Jesus
everything that I have? What keeps me
from giving him everything?

We asked Jesus for a grain of sand;
he gave us a beach.
We asked him for a drop of water;
he gave us an ocean.
We asked him for his love;
he gave us his body and blood.

*[When a woman poured expensive perfume
on Jesus' feet,
Judas criticized her, saying
that the perfume could have been sold
and the money given to the poor.]
But Jesus said, "Leave her alone! . . .
You will always have poor people with you,
but you will not always have me."*

JOHN 12:7-8

Thomas Carlyle, a 19th-century writer,
showed little affection toward his wife.
When she died, unexpectedly and suddenly,
he was plunged into deep depression.
Unable to sleep at nights,
he'd lie awake in the dark and cry out,
"Oh, if I could see her once more.
Oh, if I could tell her I loved her."

The story about Carlyle
and the story of the woman who poured
expensive perfume on Jesus' feet
invite me to inventory my expressions
of affection toward those I love.

*The worst sin
towards our fellow creatures
is not to hate them,
but to be indifferent to them:
that's the essence of inhumanity.*

GEORGE BERNARD SHAW

TUESDAY
Lent
Week 6 _____

*[Jesus] was deeply troubled
and declared openly,
"I am telling you the truth:
one of you is going to betray me."*
JOHN 13:21

Why did Judas betray Jesus?
Some think that Judas
never intended Jesus' death.
He believed that Jesus was the Messiah,
but he also believed
that the Messiah should rally the people
and drive the Romans out of Palestine.
But Jesus was not doing this.
Judas hoped that handing Jesus over
to the authorities would force him to act.
This theory would explain why Judas
took his life when things backfired.
If the theory is correct,
Judas' sin was "trying to play God."
He had his own ideas
about what the Messiah should do
and how he should go about doing it.

To what extent do I tend to play God?

*Some men die by shrapnel
And some go down in flames;
But most men perish inch by inch,
playing at little games.*
ANONYMOUS

*[While eating the Last Supper,
Jesus said to his disciples,]*
"I tell you, one of you will betray me."

MATTHEW 26:21

A letter from George Washington
to his wife is dated March 4, 1797.
It was written
shortly after his presidency ended.
Washington had been sorting papers,
deciding which to keep
and which to throw away.
He writes to his wife:
"You can imagine my feelings
as I reread Thomas Paine's last letter.
He and I were once friends . . .
and yet, because I didn't think him
qualified to become postmaster general,
he charged me with being 'treacherous.'"
Like Jesus,
Washington was deeply anguished
at having a friend turn against him.
But he had to do what was right.

To what extent do I let friendships
keep me from doing what is right?

*Anyone can stand up to an opponent:
give me someone
who can stand up to a friend.*

WILLIAM GLADSTONE (slightly adapted)

THURSDAY
Lent
Week 6 _____

[At the Last Supper, Jesus said,]
"I, your Lord and Teacher,
have just washed your feet. . . .
I have set an example for you,
so that you will do
just what I have done for you."

JOHN 13:14-15

A group of Chinese Christians
invited an American biblical scholar
to come to China to give a workshop
on Scripture.
In the course of the workshop,
the scholar asked the participants
to select the episode in the Gospel
that impressed them most.
To his surprise, the Chinese Christians
did not pick the Sermon on the Mount,
the crucifixion of Jesus, or
the resurrection of Jesus.
Rather, they picked
Jesus' washing of his disciples' feet.

What does the "washing of the feet"
say to me about Jesus? How might I
imitate Jesus' "feet-washing" action?

I may have all the faith needed
to move mountains—
but if I have no love, I am nothing.

1 CORINTHIANS 13:2

[They came to Golgotha.]
There they crucified [Jesus].
JOHN 19:18

"[Jesus] never wrote a book. . . .
He never owned a home. . . .
He never traveled two hundred miles
from the place where he was born. . . .
While still a young man,
the tide of popular opinion
turned against him. . . .
He was nailed to a cross. . . .
When he was dead, he was taken down
and laid in a borrowed grave. . . .
Nineteen centuries have come and gone,
and today he is the central figure
of the human race. . . .
I am far within the mark when I say
that all the armies that ever marched . . .
have not affected
the life of man upon earth
as powerfully as this One Solitary Life."
ANONYMOUS

What have I done for Christ?
What am I doing for Christ?
What ought I to do for Christ?

We get no deeper into Christ
than we allow him to get in us.
CHARLES SPURGEON

SATURDAY
Lent
Week 6 _____

[On Easter morning,
some women went to the tomb of Jesus.
An angel met them, saying,]
"He is not here; he has been raised,
just as he said. . . .
Go quickly, now, and tell his disciples."

MATTHEW 28:6-7

Jesus' resurrection
invites us to open our hearts
to the miracle of a new life.
It invites us to allow Jesus to do for us
what he has done for billions before us.
It invites us to love again
after our love has been rejected.
It invites us to trust again
after our trust been betrayed.
It invites us to believe again
after our faith has been shaken.
The good news of Easter is
that Jesus is alive and in our midst.
The good news of Easter is
that Jesus wants to work miracles in us.

What miracle do I want Jesus to work
in me on Easter?

Jesus' power working in us
is able to do so much more
than we can ask for, or even think of.

EPHESIANS 3:20

SEASON
OF
EASTER

SUNDAY

Easter

*[When John looked into the empty tomb
of Jesus,] he saw and believed.*

JOHN 20:8

A high school student writes:
"I had just finished my paper route
on Easter morning.
As I passed Saint Gall's church,
the sun was coming up.
I didn't intend to go in for Mass,
because I was in the midst
of a teenage rejection of the Church.
Then it happened!
The sun hit the big silver cross
in front of the church.
I couldn't take my eyes off it.
Its fiery brightness made me realize
how the apostles must have felt
on the first Easter. An unseen force
directed my feet up the church steps.
I went in, knelt down, and prayed.
For the first time in my life,
I understood what Easter was all about."
(slightly adapted)

What does Easter mean to me?
What was my most memorable Easter?

*The Gospels do not explain Easter;
Easter explains the Gospels.*

J.S. WHALE (slightly adapted)

MONDAY
Easter
Week 1 _____

[The women left Jesus' tomb] in a hurry,
afraid and yet filled with joy,
and [they] ran to tell his disciples.

MATTHEW 28:8

One of the most convincing proofs
of the resurrection
is the transformation that took place
in Jesus' followers after it.
"Off they went with burning urgency
to tell the news to all the world.
The Messiah had come.
Truly the Kingdom of God was at hand.
Their lives were led for that end,
and for that end alone.
No amount of persecution
could stop them."

B. F. RHEIN

To what extent do I feel an "urgency"
to share the good news of Jesus
with others? With whom, especially?

The lives [of Jesus' followers] . . .
changed the course of human history.
No reasonable explanation
has ever been given
to account for their transformed lives
except their own:
they had seen Jesus alive.

ROBERT L. CLEATH

[Jesus said to Mary Magdalene,]
"Do not hold on to me. . . .
But go to my brothers and tell them
that I am returning to him
who is my Father and their Father,
my God and their God."

JOHN 20:17

A mother had just returned home
from driving her only son to college.
She began to cry,
realizing that his new world
would never be her world—their world.
After the pain of separation wore off,
however, she made a big discovery.
By "letting go" of her son,
she found that she could love him
in a whole new way—
a more fulfilling way, an adult way.
Mary Magdalene
discovered the same thing
after she "let go" of the earthly Jesus
and began to relate to the risen Jesus.

What might I be holding on to
that, perhaps, I should let go of?

That which you cannot let go of,
you do not possess.
It possesses you.

IVERN BALL (slightly adapted)

WEDNESDAY
Easter
Week 1 _____

*[Two brokenhearted disciples, unaware that
Jesus had risen, were returning home
to Emmaus on Easter Sunday morning.
Jesus drew near and walked with them.
He talked to them about the Scriptures,
but they did not recognize him.
When they got to Emmaus,
the two men invited Jesus in to eat.]
He sat down . . . took the bread,
and said the blessing; then he broke
the bread and gave it to them . . .
and they recognized him.*   LUKE 24:30-31

In the resurrection stories the disciples
consistently failed to recognize Jesus
when he appeared to them.
Magdalene thought he was a gardener.
The Emmaus disciples
thought he was a lonely traveler.
The disciples on the seashore
thought he was a beachcomber.

How hard is it for me to recognize
the risen Jesus in our world? Why?

*Three things in the Emmaus story
contributed to the recognition of Jesus:
the broken hearts of the two disciples,
the broken word of the Scriptures,
the broken bread of the Eucharist.*

*[Suddenly Jesus appeared
to his disciples in the upper room.]
They were terrified,
thinking that they were seeing a ghost.
But he said to them . . .
"Look at my hands and my feet,
and see that it is I myself. . . ."
They still could not believe,
they were so full of joy and wonder.*

LUKE 24:37–39, 41

In his book *But That I Can Believe,*
John A. Robinson describes
how the disciples must have felt
before and after Jesus appeared to them:
"Jesus was someone they had known
and loved and lost. . . . It was all over. . . .
And then it happened. . . .
The life they had known and shared
was not buried with him,
but alive in them.
Jesus was not a dead memory,
but a living presence."

Where and when do I sometimes
experience the living presence of Jesus?

*"Where two or three come together
in my name,
I am there with them."*

MATTHEW 18:20

FRIDAY
Easter
Week 1 _____

[One of Jesus' Easter appearances
was to disciples on the seashore.
They were in a boat, fishing.
Standing on the beach was Jesus.
The disciples didn't recognize him at first.
Jesus yelled to them to lower their nets.
They did and made a great catch.]
Peter . . . dragged the net ashore
full of big fish,
a hundred and fifty-three in all;
even though there were so many,
still the net did not tear.
JOHN 21:11

The number 153 seems to be significant.
Ancient zoologists said there were
153 different fish in the world.
The number is thought to be symbolic
of all the nations of the world.
Likewise, the net seems to be symbolic,
standing for the Church,
which is destined to embrace
all the nations of the world.

What is one way I might contribute to
the bringing of the good news of Jesus
to all the nations of the world?

[Our job] is not to do something
for the Church,
but to do something with it.
JOSEPH F. NEWTON

[On another occasion,]
Jesus appeared to the eleven disciples
as they were eating. . . .
He said to them,
"Go throughout the whole world
and preach the gospel to all mankind."

MARK 16:14-15

The capital of Texas is named after
Stephen Austin, an early pioneer,
who founded many settlements in Texas.
Austin didn't like preachers
because they condemned his saloons
and the crime they spawned.
One man who knew Austin well
quoted him as saying that one preacher
could stir up more trouble
than a dozen horse thieves.

The story of Austin reminds us
that Jesus intended his disciples
to stir up trouble—to war against evil.
Jesus said, "I did not come to bring peace,
but a sword" (MATTHEW 10:34).
What is one way
that I could play a more active role
in the war against evil?

No one ever made more trouble
than the "gentle Jesus, meek and mild."

JAMES M. GILLIS

SUNDAY
Easter
Week 2 _____

[Thomas was absent
when Jesus appeared to the disciples.
And he refused to believe, saying,]
"Unless I see the scars of the nails
in his hands and put my finger
on those scars and my hand in his side,
I will not believe."
[Later, Jesus reappeared.
This time Thomas was there,
and Jesus said to him,]
"Reach out your hand and put it in my side.
Stop your doubting and believe!"

JOHN 20:25, 27

"Pigeon Feathers" is a story about a boy
who begins to have doubts about Jesus.
One night in bed,
the boy decides upon an experiment.
He lifts his hand above his head and
asks Jesus to touch it. Then he waits.
After a while he puts his hands down again,
not sure if Jesus touched him or not.

We all crave assurance of our faith.
In the end, however, faith is saying
to Jesus, "I trust you!"
Why do I find it hard to trust Jesus?

Sorrow looks back,
worry looks around, faith looks up.
ANONYMOUS

[Jesus said to Nicodemus,]
"No one can enter the Kingdom of God
unless he is born of water and the Spirit.
A person is born physically
of human parents,
but he is born spiritually of the Spirit."

JOHN 3:5-6

George Foreman,
former heavyweight boxing champion,
had been attending Bible classes
and was in a prayer group.
But he seemed to have no spiritual life.
One night after a fight,
he sat in the dressing room
with his head in his hands.
Suddenly he noticed blood
from a cut in his head,
dripping through his hands
onto his bare feet. Then it hit him.
These were the bloody wounds of Jesus:
head, feet, and hands.
That unusual thought was the start
of a spiritual rebirth for him.

What was an especially memorable moment
in my own spiritual life?

The person
who isn't busy being born is busy dying.

BOB DYLAN (slightly adapted)

[Jesus said about the Holy Spirit,]
"The wind blows wherever it wishes;
you hear the sound it makes,
but you do not know
where it comes from or where it is going."

JOHN 3:8

A town drunk underwent a conversion.
An old crony ridiculed him, saying,
"Surely you don't believe all that stuff
about Jesus turning water into wine?"
The ex-drunk said, "I don't know
if Jesus did that or not, but I do know
that he turned wine into food
in my house."
This fits Jesus' point when he says
that we can't see the wind,
but we can hear the sound it makes.
In other words, we can't understand
the Holy Spirit, but we can understand
the Spirit's impact on our lives.

How has the Spirit affected my life—
or the life of someone I know about?

"I will lead my blind people
by roads they have never traveled.
I will turn their darkness into light. . . .
These are my promises,
and I will keep them without fail."

ISAIAH 42:16

*God loved the world so much
that he gave his only Son,
so that everyone who believes in him
may not die but have eternal life.*

JOHN 3:16

When a friend asked 80-year-old
John Quincy Adams how he was,
he replied, "John is very well, thank you.
But the house he lives in
is sadly dilapidated.
It is tottering on its foundations.
The walls are badly shattered
and the roof is worn.
The building trembles with every wind,
and I think John Quincy Adams
will have to move out of it before long.
But he himself is very well, thank you."

To what degree is my faith
as strong as John Quincy Adam's faith?
How might I make it stronger?

*We know
that when this tent we live in—
our body here on earth—is torn down,
God will have
a house in heaven for us to live in,
a home he himself has made,
which will last forever.*

2 CORINTHIANS 5:1

THURSDAY
Easter
Week 2 _____

Whoever believes in the Son
has eternal life;
whoever disobeys the Son
will not have life.

JOHN 3:36

Mike Moran was a Navy helicopter pilot.
One day, while explaining his "chopper"
to his parents, he said,
"As complex as those machines are,
their whirling rotors are held in place
by one simple hexagonal nut."
Then turning to his mother, he said,
"Guess what that nut is called, Mom?"
She shrugged. He smiled and said,
"It's called a 'Jesus Nut.'"

To what extent
does Jesus hold my life together?
What is one area of my life
that is still not under his control?
What is one step that I might take
to begin to let Jesus take control
of this area of my life?

To the preacher who kept saying,
"We must put God in our lives,"
the Master said,
"God is already there.
Our business is to recognize this."

ANTHONY DE MELLO, S.J.

*[A large crowd was listening to Jesus.
The hour was late, and they were hungry.
A boy gave Jesus the bread and fish
that he had been saving to eat.]*
Jesus took the bread, gave thanks to God,
and distributed it to the people. . . .
He did the same with the fish,
and they all had as much as they wanted.

JOHN 6:11

At a youth rally in Scotland,
Pope John Paul II challenged
the young people to do what the boy did.
The pope invited them to offer Jesus
their lives and talents (bread and fish).
He said, "You feel conscious
of your inadequacy. . . .
But what I say to you is this:
place your lives in the hands of Jesus.
He will accept you and bless you . . .
beyond your greatest expectations."

How trustingly am I ready to place
my life and my talents (bread and fish)
in Jesus' hands?

*Blessed are they
who place themselves in the hands
of Jesus.
He will place himself in their hands.*

ANONYMOUS

SATURDAY
Easter
Week 2 _____

*[The disciples were crossing the lake
at night when a storm blew up.
Jesus came to them across the water.
They were utterly terrified.]*
"Don't be afraid," Jesus told them,
"it is I!"   JOHN 6:20

A poem describes a person in a dream,
walking along a beach with the Lord.
Suddenly, events from the person's life
flash across the sky.
Looking back at the footprints in the sand,
the person sees that during happy times
two sets of footprints appear on the sand.
But during sad times, only one set appears.
The person says to the Lord,
"I don't understand why, in times
when I need you most, you would leave."
The Lord said, "I would never leave you
during your times of trial and suffering.
When you see only one set of footprints,
it was then that I carried you."

When in my life has the Lord carried me?

Who never ate bread in sorrow,
Who never spent the darksome hours
Weeping and watching for the morrow
He knows you not, you heavenly Powers.
                    JOHANN WOLFGANG VON GOETHE

[Two totally discouraged disciples
were returning home to Emmaus on Easter.
They were unaware that Jesus had risen.
Suddenly Jesus came alongside them,
but they didn't recognize him.
They figured he was just a stranger
who wanted company. When they got to Emmaus,
they asked him in for supper.]
He sat down to eat with them,
took the bread, and said the blessing;
then he broke the bread and gave it to them.
Then their eyes were opened
and they recognized him. LUKE 24:30-31

Noreen Towers was working among the poor
with no evident success.
One night she went to bed very discouraged.
The next morning, shortly after waking,
Jesus seemed to speak to her, saying,
"Can you not trust my plan for you?"
That split-second experience
changed her from a defeated person
into a person with unshakeable faith.

What did I learn
from a discouraging moment in my life?

How else but through a broken heart
May the Lord Christ enter in?
OSCAR WILDE

MONDAY
Easter
Week 3 _____

[Jesus said,]
"Do not work for food that spoils;
instead, work for the food
that lasts for eternal life."

JOHN 6:27

Boxer Jack Dempsey went to bed
around 2 A.M. the night he won
the world's heavyweight championship.
An hour later, he woke with a start.
He had just dreamt that he had lost
his newly won championship.
Unable to get back to sleep,
he went out and bought some newspapers
to see what they said about the fight.
"Reading through the accounts,"
he said later, "I began to realize
that success didn't taste
the way I thought it would. . . .
I was left with a curious feeling
of emptiness."

Dempsey's experience invites me to ask:
Do I ever experience "a curious feeling
of emptiness" about my life?

[Jesus warned,]
"This is how it is with those
who pile up riches for themselves
but are not rich in God's sight."

LUKE 12:21

"I am the bread of life," Jesus [said.]
"He who comes to me will never be hungry."

JOHN 6:35

In the 1800s an immigrant family
spent almost all its money
for boat tickets to the United States.
To save the little money they had left,
they remained in their cabin and ate
hard bread and water, rather than go
to the ship's dining room
with its more expensive food.
When they docked in New York,
they learned the ship's meals were free.
They were included in the ticket price.

Many people
voyage through life in a similar way.
They starve "spiritually,"
rather than eat the "bread of life,"
free at every Lord's Supper.
What is my experience of the Lord's Supper
at this juncture in my life?
What might I do to deepen and enrich
that experience?

The effect of our sharing
in the body and blood of Christ
is to change us
into what we receive.

POPE SAINT LEO THE GREAT

WEDNESDAY
Easter
Week 3 _____

*[Jesus said,] "What my Father wants
is that all who see the Son and believe
in him should have eternal life."*

JOHN 6:40

More than any other scientist,
Wernher von Braun was responsible
for putting America on the moon.
Before he died, he gave this testimony
concerning life after death:
"I think science has a real surprise
for the skeptics. . . . Nothing in nature,
not even the tiniest particle,
can disappear without a trace.
Nature does not know extinction.
All it knows is transformation. . . .
Everything science has taught me—
and continues to teach me—
strengthens my belief in the continuity
of our spiritual existence after death."

Why don't I live more in accord
with my belief that this life is only
the launching pad for eternal life?

*If I find in myself a desire
that no experience in this world
can satisfy,
the most probable explanation is
that I was made for another world.*

C. S. LEWIS

*[Jesus said,] "He who is from God
is the only one who has seen the Father."*

JOHN 6:46

A college girl said in a discussion,
"I cannot believe in God any longer."
Her professor replied,
"Maybe I should congratulate you."
"What do you mean?" she asked.
Her professor replied,
"Perhaps the idea of God that you reject
should be rejected."
The professor's point is important.
Often the "god" that people reject
is not the true God,
but an erroneous notion of God
that exists only in their minds.

The clearest image of God
is to be found in Jesus, who said,
"Whoever has seen me
has seen the Father" (JOHN 14:9).
What is there about Jesus
that speaks to me most eloquently
about the Father?

*As the print of the seal on wax
is the express image of the seal itself,
so Christ is the express image—
the perfect representation of God.*

SAINT AMBROSE

FRIDAY
Easter
Week 3 _____

*[Jesus said,] "If you do not eat the flesh
of the Son of Man and drink his blood,
you will not have life in yourselves.
Whoever eats my flesh and drinks my blood
has eternal life."*   JOHN 6:53-54

Advertising executive Emilie Griffin
was brought up a Christian Scientist.
But when she reached adulthood,
she experienced a faith struggle.
It is described in her book *Turning*.
A major focus of her struggle
was Jesus' statement
that his body and his blood
were real food and real drink—
a statement that infuriated his enemies
and caused many disciples to leave him
(JOHN 6:32, 66). Eventually, Emilie's faith
in Jesus' "real presence" in the Eucharist
led her to embrace the Church.

Emilie's faith in the Eucharist
invites me to inventory my own faith in
and devotion to the Eucharist.

> *INVITATION*
> *Jesus of Nazareth*
> *requests the honor of your presence*
> *at a meal to be given in his honor.*
>   ANONYMOUS

*[After Jesus said he would give
his body as food and his blood as drink,
many of his followers left him.]
So he asked the twelve disciples,
"And you—would you also like to leave?"
Simon Peter answered him,
"Lord, to whom would we go?
You have the words that give eternal life.
And now we believe and know
that you are the Holy One
who has come from God."* JOHN 6:67-69

At a Fellowship of Christian Athletes
breakfast in New Orleans,
sportscaster Gary Bender suggested
five things that Jesus might say
to you or me if he appeared to us today:

1. I love you;
2. I know you;
3. I understand you;
4. I forgive you.
5. Do you know me?

Bender's words invite me to ask:
How well do I know Jesus?
How might I get to know him better?

*To be ignorant of the Scriptures
is to be ignorant of Christ.*
SAINT JEROME

SUNDAY
Easter
Week 4 _____

*[Jesus said,] "I have come
in order that you might have life—
life in all its fullness."*

JOHN 10:10

A woman was diagnosed
as being terminally ill.
For a while, she continued to live
pretty much as she always did.
Then, one day, she said to herself,
"What am I doing?
What am I building a bank account for?
What am I living this way for?"
Then she decided to begin living
as her heart dictated.
That woman lived 15 more months.
Before she died,
she confided to a friend,
"The last 15 months of my life
were the richest of my entire life."

The woman's experience invites me to ask:
What was one of the richest periods
of my entire life?

*I shall pass through this world but once.
Any good that I can do, or any kindness
that I can show to any human being,
let me do it now and not defer it.
For I shall not pass this way again.*

Attributed to STEPHEN GRELLET (adapted)

137

[Jesus said,] "I am the good shepherd.
As the Father knows me . . .
in the same way
I know my sheep and they know me.
And I am willing to die for them."

JOHN 10:14-15

A young shepherd
was grazing his flock near Mount Tabor.
Suddenly three Bedouin outlaws appeared.
The shepherd knew the danger he was in,
but he stood his ground
and fought to keep his flock.
The episode ended with the shepherd
being knifed to death
as he attempted to protect his flock.
Jesus had an image like this in mind
when he said, "I am the good shepherd. . . .
And I am willing to die for [the sheep]"
(JOHN 10:14-15).

The story of the young shepherd
invites me to ask:
What is one heroic thing
I was called upon to do in my life?
What motivated me to do it?
How do I look back upon it now?

Plunge into the deep without fear,
with the gladness of April in your heart.

RABINDRANATH TAGORE

TUESDAY
Easter
Week 4 _____

[Jesus said,]
"My sheep listen to my voice;
I know them, and they follow me . . .
and they shall never die."

JOHN 10:27-28

In World War II, Flying Fortresses
flew from the United States
to the island of Saipan in the Pacific.
Each plane was met by a little Jeep
with a sign reading: "Follow Me!"
The Jeep then led the giant plane
to its assigned parking spot
on the island's airstrip.
A young pilot said of the Jeep:
"I'm not very religious,
but that little Jeep, with its quaint sign,
always reminds me of Jesus.
He was a little, scrawny peasant,
but the giant men and women of our time
would be lost without his direction."

What is one thing that keeps me
from following Jesus more closely than I do?
What might Jesus say to me about it?

The living Christ still has two hands,
one to point the way,
and the other held out
to help us along the way.

T. W. MASON

*[Jesus said,] "Whoever rejects me
and does not accept my message
has one who will judge him.
The words I have spoken
will be his judge on the last day!"*

JOHN 12:48

W. C. Fields was a great film comedian.
A story—probably apocryphal—
says that near the end of his life
he spent a lot of time
reading the Bible.
Someone asked him about this,
and Fields replied, "I'm looking
for any loopholes I can find."
The implication was that Fields knew
that he had not lived his life
in full accord with Jesus' teaching.
Now he was looking for a way
to excuse himself for this failure
when he appeared before God.

If I died and appeared before God tonight,
what excuse would I give
for not having lived in fuller accord
with Jesus' teaching?

*If Christ were standing
before me now, what would I feel,
not about him, but about myself?*

SAINT AUGUSTINE (slightly adapted)

THURSDAY
Easter
Week 4 _____

*[At the Last Supper, Jesus prayed
to his Father for his disciples, saying,]
"I sent them into the world,
just as you sent me"* (JOHN 17:18).
*[Jesus assured his disciples,]
"Whoever receives anyone I send
receives me also;
and whoever receives me
receives him who sent me."*

JOHN 13:20

A college girl told a friend,
"I believe in God,
and I believe Jesus is God's Son,
but I don't believe in the Church."
Her friend said, "But that's impossible!
You can't separate Jesus and the Church.
They are one—
just as Jesus and the Father are one.
The Holy Spirit came on Pentecost
and formed Jesus and his disciples
into a single body, the Church."
(EPHESIANS 1:23)

To what extent do I tend to separate
Jesus from his Church? Why?

*You cannot have God for your Father,
if you don't have the Church
for your mother.*

SAINT AUGUSTINE

*[Shortly before returning to his Father,
Jesus said to his disciples,]*
*"I am going to prepare a place for you.
I would not tell you this
if it were not so. And after I go
and prepare a place for you,
I will come back and take you to myself,
so that you will be where I am."*

JOHN 14:2-3

John Peterson
wrote a hymn about heaven.
A portion of its lyrics read:
"Over the sunset mountains,
Heaven awaits for me;
Over the sunset mountains,
Jesus my Savior I'll see."
A music critic told Peterson,
"Skip the notion of being with Jesus
and spend more time
describing the joy of heaven."
Of course, Peterson refused,
because the essence of heaven's joy
is standing face-to-face with Jesus.

How comfortable am I with the thought
of standing face-to-face with Jesus?

*The goal of religion is not to get us
into heaven—but to get heaven into us.*

ANONYMOUS

SATURDAY
Easter
Week 4 _____

[Jesus said,] "For a long time
I have been with you all;
yet you do not know me, Philip?
Whoever has seen me
has seen the Father."

JOHN 14:9

A lady asked, "How can Christians claim
to have a special knowledge of God?"
The answer, of course,
depends upon who you say Jesus is.
No bonafide religious leader
ever claimed what Jesus claimed.
Buddha rejected veneration.
Muhammad admitted being a sinner.
Jesus is the only religious leader who
dared to say, "Whoever has seen me
has seen the Father."
If Jesus is who he claimed to be,
then Christians can rightly claim
a special knowledge of God.

Thomas Carlyle said that if Jesus
came today, people wouldn't crucify him.
They'd invite him to dinner, hear what
he had to say, and make fun of it.
To what extent do I agree with Carlyle?

What am I to do with Jesus?
I have to do something with him.
I cannot ignore him.

[Jesus said,]
"I am the way, the truth, and the life;
no one goes to the Father except by me. . . .
Believe me when I say
that I am in the Father
and the Father is in me."　　JOHN 14:6, 11

In 1965 huge areas of Canada and
the United States were blacked out
by the failure of an electric fuse
the size of a football.
All power to those huge areas
funneled through that single fuse.
Later, someone compared the fuse
to Jesus, saying,
"As that tiny fuse was the passageway
by which power went forth to
the United States and Canada,
so Jesus is the tiny passageway
by which we go forth to the Father."

To what extent is my own life and faith
reflected in this statement:
"When we have traveled all ways,
we shall come to the End of all ways,
who says 'I am the way'"?　SAINT ANDREW

Jesus is the way to the Father,
the truth about the Father,
and the life of the Father.

MONDAY
Easter
Week 5 _____

[Jesus said,]
"Whoever accepts my commandments
and obeys them
is the one who loves me.
My Father will love whoever loves me."
JOHN 14:21

One character in Richard Bach's
Jonathan Livingston Seagull
is Chiang, Jonathan's teacher.
When the day comes for Chiang
to say good-bye to his young student,
Jonathan knows it is a special moment.
He wonders what parting advice
his old teacher will give him.
Chiang utters it in just five words:
"Jonathan, keep working on love."
It is this same parting advice
that Jesus gave to his own disciples:
"Keep working on love."

If I asked Jesus how his parting advice
applied to me right now in my life,
how might he answer me?

We have learned
to fly in the air like birds
and to swim in the sea like fish.
But we have not learned
the simple act of living together.
MARTIN LUTHER KING, JR.

[In a final instruction to his disciples,
Jesus said,]
"Peace is what I leave with you;
it is my own peace that I give you."

JOHN 14:27

The great musician Pablo Casals
was also a tireless worker for peace.
When he announced plans
to circle the globe in a peace crusade,
he said:
"I am a man first, an artist second.
As a man,
my first obligation is to the welfare
of my fellowman.
I will endeavor to meet this obligation
through music—
the means God has given me—
since it transcends language,
politics and national boundaries.
My contribution to world peace
may be small.
But at least I will have given all I can."

Jesus said, "Happy are those
who work for peace" (MATTHEW 5:9).
What is one way I might work for peace?

World peace begins in each heart.
If the tree is to be green,
its individual leaves must be green.

WEDNESDAY
Easter
Week 5 ——————————————

[Jesus said to his disciples,]
"You can do nothing without me.
Whoever does not remain in me
is thrown out like a branch and dries up."

JOHN 15:5-6

An old Jewish story concerns a woman
who stopped going to the synagogue.
One day the rabbi went to her house
and asked to sit with her by the fireplace.
For a long time, neither spoke.
Then the rabbi picked up a tongs,
took a glowing coal from the fireplace,
and set it on the hearth.
As the two watched,
the coal slowly lost its glow and died.
A few minutes later,
the old woman said, "I understand.
I'll come back to the synagogue."

Is there anything
that threatens to cut me off from Jesus
and cause me to lose my glow?
Is there anyone who has been cut off
from Jesus that I might help,
as the rabbi helped the old woman?

"We find comfort
among those who agree with us—
growth among those who don't."

FRANK A. CLARK

[Jesus said,]
"I love you just as the Father loves me;
remain in my love."   JOHN 15:9

A little girl was showing her dolls
to her granddmother.
Her grandmother asked her,
"Which one do you like most?"
The little girl said,
"Promise you won't laugh if I tell you."
Her grandmother promised.
Then the little girl picked up
the most miserable-looking doll of all.
"Why do you like that one most?"
asked her grandmother.
The little girl said, "Because it needs
my love more than the pretty ones do."

The little girl's love for the doll
reflects Jesus' love for us.
He loves us because we are sinners
and need his love most.
Jesus' love for us
and the girl's love for the tattered doll
invite me to ask: What is one way
that I can love more as they do?

No one needs love more
than someone who doesn't deserve it.
                                    ANONYMOUS

FRIDAY
Easter
Week 5 _____

[Jesus said,] "My commandment is this:
love one another, just as I love you."

JOHN 15:12

The British poet Leigh Hunt
wrote a poem called
"Abou ben Adhem."
One night Abou awoke and saw an angel
writing in a book the names
of those who loved God most.
Abou asked, "And is mine one?"
The angel replied, "Nay, not so."
Then Abou told the angel to write down
that he loved his fellowmen greatly.
The angel wrote and vanished.
"The next night / It came again
with a great awakening light, /
And showed the names
whom love of God had blessed, /
And lo! Ben Adhem's name
led all the rest."

If I asked the angel the same question
that Abou ben Adhem did,
how might the angel answer me?
How might I reply to the angel?

"Whenever you did this
for one of the least important . . .
you did it for me!"

MATTHEW 25:40

[Jesus said,]
"Remember what I told you:
'No slave is greater than his master.'
If they persecuted me,
they will persecute you too."

JOHN 15:20

An American warship was filled
with wounded prisoners of war.
The medical officer in charge
gave them such excellent care
that another officer complained, saying,
"Treat them the same way
that they treat our wounded."
The medical officer replied,
"I'm not going to play
by their set of rules, but by ours.
I'm going to do my best
to replace whatever hatred they have
in their hearts."

By what set of rules do I usually play:
those of Jesus,
or those of the world?
How comfortable am I in doing this?

He drew a circle that shut me out—
Heretic, rebel, a thing to flout.
But love and I had the wit to win.
We drew a circle that took him in.

EDWIN MARKHAM, "Outwitted"

SUNDAY
Easter
Week 6 _____

[Jesus said to his disciples,]
"Whoever accepts my commandments and
obeys them is the one who loves me. . . .
I too will love him
and reveal myself to him."   JOHN 14:21

An old legend tells
about an angel walking down the street,
carrying a torch in one hand
and a pail of water in the other.
"What are you going to do with those?"
someone asked. The angel replied,
"With the torch I'm going to burn down
the mansions of heaven;
and with the pail of water,
I'm going to put out the fires of hell.
Then we shall see who really loves God."
The angel's point is that many people
keep the commandments more out of
fear of punishment or hope of reward
than out of love for God.

What is the biggest reason
I keep the commandments:
fear of punishment,
hope of reward, or love of God?

The hand will not reach out for
what the heart does not long for.
                    GERMAN PROVERB

[Jesus said to his disciples,
"When the Holy Spirit comes,
you] will speak about me,
because you have been with me
from the very beginning."

JOHN 15:27

Former Penn State football star
D. J. Dozier knelt and prayed
after he scored in the Fiesta Bowl.
His action sparked instant criticism.
Coming to his defense, R. D. Lashar,
an outstanding high school kicker, said,
"Before and after each place kick,
I kneel and pray. The day someone tells me
I can't pray is the day I don't play!
It's a free country."
Sports fan Mark Roberts wrote,
"I find it refreshing to see someone
do something besides a silly dance . . .
and flaunting an oversized ego."

That I am called
to witness to Jesus is one thing.
How I witness to him is another.
What is probably the most convincing way
that I am witnessing to Jesus?

Every believer in this world
must become a spark of light.

POPE JOHN XXIII

TUESDAY
Easter
Week 6 _____

[After telling his disciples
that he was going to the Father,
Jesus said,] "Now that I have told you,
your hearts are full of sadness.
But I am telling you the truth:
it is better for you that I go away,
because if I do not go,
the Helper [Spirit] will not come to you."

JOHN 16:6-7

In *The Ultimate Seduction,*
Charlotte Chandler quotes Israeli
Prime Minister Golda Meir as saying,
"I was never a beauty. There was a time
when I was sorry about that. . . .
It was only much later
that I realized that not being beautiful
was a blessing in disguise.
It forced me to develop
my inner resources."
What often begins as a cross in life
becomes a blessing.
What begins as sadness becomes a joy.

What is one thing about myself
that I found hard to accept at first
but from which I later benefitted much?

Defeat may serve as well as victory
to shake the soul and let the glory out.

EDWIN MARKHAM

[Jesus said,]
"I have much more to tell you, but now
it would be too much for you to bear.
When, however, the Spirit comes,
who reveals the truth about God,
he will lead you into all the truth."

JOHN 16:12-13

While Kathryn Koob was a hostage in Iran,
angry mobs shouted outside her room,
almost around the clock.
One night she woke up with a start.
She says, "I turned quickly,
expecting to see one of my guards.
But no one was there."
Kathryn then adds that, for some reason,
she "was reminded of the Holy Spirit."
From then on,
the Spirit seemed to be with her in prison
in a special way.
She says, "He was teaching me love . . .
and new understanding."

In what area of my life, right now,
would I like the Holy Spirit to give me
new love and new understanding?

O Holy Spirit, Paraclete, perfect in us
the work begun by Jesus.

POPE JOHN XXIII

[Before ascending to the Father,
Jesus said to his disciples,]
"Go . . . to all peoples everywhere
and make them my disciples. . . .
And I will be with you always."

MATTHEW 28:19-20

A woman saw a little girl in the street
playing with filthy trash.
The child was poorly dressed
and ill-nourished.
The woman became angry and said to God,
"Why do you let a thing like that
happen in the world you created?
Why don't you do something about it?"
God replied, "I did do something about it;
I created you."

That story invites me to ask myself:
How seriously do I take Jesus' command
to transform our world into
the kind of place God created it to be?

The Ascension of Christ
is his liberation from all restrictions
of time and space.
It does not represent his removal
from earth,
but his constant presence everywhere
on earth.

WILLIAM TEMPLE

[Jesus said,] "Now you are sad,
but I will see you again,
and your hearts will be filled with gladness,
the kind of gladness
that no one can take away from you."

JOHN 16:22

A 13-year old girl was dead of leukemia.
While going through her belongings,
her parents found a poem
she had written during her illness.
It confirmed in a beautiful way
what Jesus says in today's gospel:
A portion of it reads:
"O God, I'm Free! . . . .
Your hand came through the dark,
A faint spark; but it lit my soul.
My fire is burning, Lord.
No one can put it out.
O God, I'm Free!"
MISSION Magazine

The girl's poem invites me to pray,
O God, show me what I can do
to help your hand come through the dark
and light a spark in another's life.

Sometimes opportunity knocks,
but most of the time it sneaks up on you
and then quietly steals away.

DOUG LARSEN

SATURDAY
Easter
Week 6 _____

[Jesus said,]
"The Father will give you
whatever you ask of him in my name.
Until now you have not asked
for anything in my name;
ask and you will receive."

JOHN 16:23-24

Roland Stair tells this story.
A hospital chaplain learned that a patient
from his hometown was in Room 164.
But when the chaplain got to the room,
the expected patient was not there.
The chaplain apologized, saying,
"I probably made a mistake."
The patient in the room replied,
"It's no mistake, your being here;
I've been praying for the courage
to talk to you.
But I couldn't bring myself to do it.
And now you wander in here by mistake.
No, it was no mistake!"

What is one thing in my life that I would
like to do but lack the courage to do?
What is one thing I might do
to break through this situation?

Work as if everything depends on you.
Pray as if everything depends on God.
SAINT IGNATIUS OF LOYOLA

[Jesus prayed to his Father,]
"Eternal life means
to know you, the only true God, and
to know Jesus Christ, whom you sent."

JOHN 17:3

Mark Twain's wit and charm
made him popular not only in America
but also in Europe.
On one European trip, he was invited
to dine with a head of state.
When Twain's little daughter
learned of the invitation, she said,
"Daddy, you know every big person
there is to know, except God."
She was referring to the fact
that her daddy was not a religious man,
at least in the formal sense.

An example of Twain's irreligious wit
is this sentence from his *Notebook:*
"If Christ were here now,
there is one thing he would not be—
a Christian."
What is Twain's point
and to what extent might it be valid today?

Religion is not a way of looking
at certain things. It is a certain way
of looking at everything.

ROBERT E. SEGAL

MONDAY
Easter
Week 7 _____

[Jesus said,]
"The time is coming . . .
when all of you will be scattered,
each one to his own home. . . .
The world will make you suffer.
But be brave!
I have defeated the world!"

JOHN 16:32-33

Jesus probably noticed the fear
on his disciples' faces when he told them
that they would have to suffer.
But their fear did not alarm Jesus.
He knew that fear is not a bad thing.
If used properly, it is a good thing.
Test pilot Chuck Yeager says:
"You feed off fear
as if it's a high-energy candy bar.
It keeps you focused and alert."
This is also the reasoning
behind Starbuck's comment
in *Moby Dick*, when he says
that the only men he wants in his boat
are men who are afraid of whales.

When was I really afraid in my life?
What do I fear most, right now?

Courage is being scared to death—
but saddling up anyway.

ACTOR JOHN WAYNE

TUESDAY
Easter
Week 7

*Jesus . . . looked up to heaven
and said,
"Father, the hour has come. . . .
I have finished the work
you gave me to do. . . .
I have made you known
to those you gave me."*

JOHN 17:1, 4, 6

This picture of Jesus at prayer recalls
an episode from Dorothy Day's life.
She says that before her conversion
and her work among New York's poor,
she often spent the night in taverns.
Then, on her way home,
around six o'clock in the morning,
she would stop in at St. Joseph's Church
on Sixth Avenue.
What attracted her to St. Joseph's
was the sight of the people praying
at early Mass. She writes:
"I longed for their faith. . . .
So I used to go in and kneel in the back."

Can I recall a time when I was moved
by the faith of people at prayer?

*If you Christians in India, in Britain,
or in America were like your Bible,
you would conquer India in five years.*

INDIAN BRAHMAN TO A MISSIONARY

WEDNESDAY
Easter
Week 7

[Jesus prayed for his disciples, saying,]
"Holy Father! . . .
I gave them your message. . . .
I sent them into the world,
just as you sent me into the world.
And for their sake I dedicate myself to you,
in order that they, too,
may be truly dedicated to you."

JOHN 17:11, 14, 18-19

Legend says that when Jesus returned
to heaven, the angel Gabriel asked him
if all people knew of his love for them.
"Oh, no!" said Jesus, "only a handful do."
Gabriel was shocked and asked,
"How will the rest learn?"
Jesus said, "The *handful* will tell them."
"But," said Gabriel,
"What if they let you down?
What if they meet opposition?
What if they become discouraged?
Don't you have a back-up plan?"
"No," said Jesus, "I'm counting on them
not to let me down."

What convinces me
that Jesus' followers won't let him down?

I used to ask God to help me.
Then I asked if I might help him.

HUDSON TAYLOR

[Jesus spoke to his Father
about his disciples in these words:]
"I pray not only for them,
but also for those who believe in me
because of their message.
I pray that they may all be one."

JOHN 17:20-21

Nobel Prize winner Alexis Carrel writes:
"When we pray we link ourselves
to the inexhaustible motive power
which spins the universe.
We ask that a part of this power
be apportioned to our needs.
Even in asking,
our deficiencies are filled and
we rise strengthened and refreshed. . . .
True prayer is a way of life.
The truest life is literally
a life of prayer."

What is one way that prayer
has had an effect on my life
since I began praying regularly?

Prayer is like the turning on
of an electric switch.
It does not create the current;
it simply provides a channel
through which the current can flow.

MAX HANDEL

FRIDAY
Easter
Week 7 _____

[Three times Jesus asked Simon Peter,]
"Simon son of John, do you love me?"
[Three times Peter responded,]
"Yes, Lord . . .
you know that I love you."
[Three times Jesus commissioned Peter,
saying,] "Take care of my sheep."

JOHN 21:16

Peter's triple affirmation of love
erased his triple denial of Jesus,
which he uttered the night before Jesus
was crucified (MARK 14:72).
And Jesus' triple response to Peter
commissioned Peter to succeed him
as shepherd of the flock
of his followers on earth.

What is my attitude toward the shepherds
of God's flock on earth today?
What one thing, especially, helps me
to see beyond their human weaknesses
to the commission Jesus gave them?

[The Church] is a society of sinners.
It is the only society in the world
in which membership
is based upon a single qualification,
that the candidate be unworthy
of membership.

CHARLES CLAYTON MORRISON

Now, there are many other things
that Jesus did.
If they were all written down one by one,
I suppose that the whole world
could not hold the books
that would be written. JOHN 21:25

A pickup truck pulled off the road.
A voice from the cab yelled to
a bunch of Boy Scouts in the back:
"Prayer time. Finish your rosaries
while I finish my office."
(The office is a book of daily prayer
made up mainly of scripture readings.)
Father Joyce sat next to the headlight
and began praying his office.
Almost immediately, a rig rolled up
and the driver said, "Need any help?"
"No," said Father Joyce, "just reading!"
As the rig rolled off, the priest smiled
at the trucker's parting words:
"Must be a darn good book!"

What story/passage in the "good book"
speaks to me in a special way? Why?

I know the Bible is inspired
because it finds me at a greater depth
of my being than any other book.
SAMUEL TAYLOR COLERIDGE

SUNDAY

Pentecost _____

[Jesus breathed on his disciples
and said,] "Receive the Holy Spirit."

JOHN 20:22

The Cross and the Switchblade
describes Rev. David Wilkerson's work
with young derelicts in New York City.
One firsthand report in the book
comes from a heroin user named Joe.
He says: "The Holy Spirit
is called the Comforter, they told me.
When I thought of comfort, I thought of
a bottle of wine and a dozen goof balls.
But these guys
were talking about comfort from heaven
where I could feel clean later.
I got to wanting this. . . .
I cried to God for help and that's when
he [the Holy Spirit] came. . . .
I didn't want any more drugs.
I loved everybody. For the first time
in my life I felt clean."

What role does the Holy Spirit play
in my life?
Do I pray to the Holy Spirit?

O come, O Holy Spirit, come!
Come as holy light and lead us.
Come as holy truth and teach us.

ANCIENT PRAYER (adapted)

_____ SPECIAL NOTE

Starting today (Monday), the *Lectionary*
readings vary from year to year. To
determine the reflection exercise to use
today,

- locate the current year,
- read across to the week and page,
- turn to them and begin.

This will put you in the correct sequence
for the rest of the year. (For example, if the
year is 1995, begin with Week 9, page 225.)

Year	Week	Page
1992	10	232
1993	9	225
1994	8	218
1995	9	225
1996	8	218
1997	7	211
1998	9	225
1999	8	218
2000	10	232
2001	9	225
2002	7	211
2003	10	232
2004	9	225
2005	7	211
2006	9	225
2007	8	218
2008	6	204
2009	9	225
2010	8	218

SEASON OF ORDINARY TIME

SUNDAY (Lord's Baptism)
Ordinary Time
Week 1

As soon as Jesus was baptized,
he came up out of the water.
Then heaven was opened to him,
and he saw the Spirit of God coming down
like a dove and lighting on him.
Then a voice said from heaven,
"This is my own dear Son,
with whom I am pleased."

MATTHEW 3:16-17

Old Testament writers
called someone a "son of God"
much as we call a good person an "angel."
In other words, they used the title
in a figurative sense.
Thus, they called kings "sons of God."
New Testament writers, on the other hand,
reserved the title for Jesus.
They used it in a *literal* sense
because that is how they experienced Jesus:
"as the Father's only Son" (JOHN 1:14).

What convinces me most
that Jesus is "the Father's only Son"?

The Son of God died;
it is by all means to be believed
because it is absurd.
And he was buried and rose again;
it is certain because it is impossible.

TERTULLIAN (ca.A.D. 200)

MONDAY
Ordinary Time
Week 1 _____

Jesus . . . saw two fishermen, Simon and
his brother Andrew, catching fish. . . .
Jesus said to them, "Come with me,
and I will teach you to catch men." . . .
They left their nets and went with him.

Mark 1:16-18

Mother Teresa was about 40 years old
when Jesus called her to her new work.
She went to the slums of Calcutta
to care for the poorest of the poor.
Soon other women joined her.
The result? A new religious order of women,
the Missionary Sisters of Charity,
was founded.
Today, while other orders decline,
Mother Teresa's order draws thousands.
If you touch people's hearts
and give them a noble challenge,
they will flock to your side.
That's what made them flock to Jesus.

How open am I to embarking upon
an apostolic undertaking with Jesus?
What are some reservations I have?

Treat people as if they were
what they ought to be,
and you will help them to become
what they are capable of being.
JOHANN WOLFGANG VON GOETHE

TUESDAY
Ordinary Time
Week 1

*[One day Jesus expelled an evil spirit
from a person.] The people were all
so amazed that they started saying
to one another, "What is this? . . .
This man has authority to give orders
to the evil spirits, and they obey him!"*

MARK 1:27

A popular word for a "miracle"
is the Greek work *semion,* meaning "sign."
(The evangelists wrote in Greek.)
This word indicates that Jesus' miracles
were like flashing red lights.
The important thing is not
the flashing light, but what it means.
In other words, what did Jesus intend
a particular miracle to signify?
For example,
when Jesus drove out evil spirits,
it signified that the kingdom of Satan
was giving way to the Kingdom of God.

God's Kingdom, which Jesus began,
is like a planted seed. Jesus sowed it.
But we must cultivate it
if it is to bear its intended fruit.
What is one way I can help cultivate it?

*Each one has a mission to fulfill,
a mission of love.*

MOTHER TERESA

Simon's mother-in-law
was sick in bed with a fever,
and as soon as Jesus arrived,
he was told about her.
He went to her, took her by the hand,
and helped her up. The fever left her,
and she began to wait on them.

MARK 1:30-31

A speeding train struck a car driven
by a University of Cincinnati student.
Miraculously, the student was uninjured.
The event affected the student deeply.
She no longer felt her life was her own,
to do with as she pleased.
She felt that she had been saved
by no merit or skill of her own.
She believed
that she had been saved "to serve."
Peter's mother-in-law responded
in a similar way when Jesus cured her.
The Gospel says,
"She began to wait on them."

What was my closest brush with death?
How did it affect my attitude
concerning the rest of my life? Why?

You cannot just go on being a good egg.
You must either hatch or go bad.

C. S. LEWIS

[A leper asked Jesus to cure him.]
Jesus . . . reached out and touched him.
"I do want to," he answered. "Be clean!"
At once the disease left the man.

MARK 1:41–42

New York University studies show
that when nurses lay hands on patients
with the intention of healing them,
the patients' recovery accelerates.
This leads some doctors to believe
"that there is a natural power of life
in loving people
which is communicated in a special way
through the power of touch
and that the patient
absorbs much of this life, or energy,
in such a way
that the sick body can build up
its own life-building forces."
FRANCIS MACNUTT

To what extent do I express my love,
especially for family members,
in a tangible, concrete way?

Lord, help me to realize
that one warm embrace
or one loving touch of the hand
may be able to release more healing
than a bucketful of pills and medicine.

FRIDAY
Ordinary Time
Week 1 _____

[Some people
brought a paralytic to Jesus
to be healed.]
Seeing how much faith they had,
Jesus said to the paralyzed man,
"My son, your sins are forgiven."
[At once the man was healed.]

MARK 2:5

A famous singer said:
"I owe my entire career to my wife.
She had faith in me at a time
when I didn't have faith in myself."
The paralyzed man
appears to have been like the singer.
He owed his healing
to the faith of his friends.
They were the ones who believed
that Jesus could and would heal him.

I, too, have been helped
by the faith of other people.
Apart from my parents,
who is one person who has helped me
in a special way in my faith journey?

You give but little
when you give of your possessions.
It is when you give of yourself
that you truly give.

KAHLIL GIBRAN

[Jesus said,] "People who are well
do not need a doctor,
but only those who are sick.
I have not come to call respectable people,
but outcasts."   MARK 2:17

A woman bought
a beautiful old porcelain pitcher.
It was cream colored
with hand-painted flowers on it.
One day someone dropped it,
breaking it into scores of pieces.
The woman gathered them up
and began to glue them together again.
As she worked over the broken pitcher,
she thought, "This is how God labors over
broken individuals, mending them."

The people you and I tend to write off,
God labors over patiently, mending them.
Who is a person that I am tempted
to write off as beyond repair?
What is one thing I might do
to help him or her?

The Easter Message means
that God can turn prostitutes like Magdalene
into disciples . . .
and broken reeds like Simon Peter
into rocks.
                                FULTON SHEEN

SUNDAY
Ordinary Time
Week 2 _____

*[One day John the Baptist
was talking with some people.
Seeing Jesus in the distance,
he said,] "There is the Lamb of God,
who takes away the sin of the world!
This is the one I was talking about."*

JOHN 1:29-30

John the Baptist touched people's hearts
for two reasons:
he helped them to see they were sinners
who needed a savior;
and he helped them to open their hearts
to Jesus, who came to save them.

This raises two questions for me.
To what extent do I see myself
as a sinner who needs a savior?
And to what extent am I opening my heart
to Jesus, who came to save me?

*Many people do not recognize Christ
because they do not recognize themselves
as sinners. If I am not a sinner,
I have no need of Christ.
I won't celebrate the mystery of Christ
in joy if I don't realize in sorrow
that I am a sinner who needs a savior.
The focus, however, is not on sin,
but on Christ who saves.*

KILIAN MCDONNELL (slightly adapted)

*[Some people complained to Jesus
because his disciples no longer observed
certain traditions. Jesus responded,]
"No one uses a piece of new cloth
to patch up an old coat,
because the new patch will shrink
and tear off some of the old cloth,
making an even bigger hole."*

MARK 2:21

In 1876 Western Union officials dismissed
the telephone as a "toy."
In 1878 the British Parliament ridiculed Edison's
experiments on an electric light.
In 1945 Admiral Leahy called the atom bomb
a "fool thing" that wouldn't work.
These examples illustrate why some people
rejected Jesus' teaching.
They had become so wedded to the status quo
that they had become blind
to new visions and new possibilities.

These examples invite me to recall
a time when I resisted a certain change,
only to learn later
that it was the best thing
that could have happened to me.

*I can think of only one person
who welcomes change—a wet baby.*
AUTHOR UNKNOWN

TUESDAY
Ordinary Time
Week 2 _____

*[One day some Pharisees rebuked Jesus
because his followers
did not keep certain Sabbath laws.
Jesus said to them,]*
*"The Sabbath was made for the good of man;
man was not made for the Sabbath."*

MARK 2:27

The movie *The Snake Pit*
concerns the fate of the mentally ill
in old-fashioned "insane asylums."
In one scene, someone buys a small rug
for the asylum's recreation room.
But the attendants of the asylum
make the patients walk around the rug
to keep it from getting dirty.
So the patients always circle around it.
The whole purpose of the rug is lost.
Jesus makes a similar point.
He reminds the Pharisees
that the law was made to serve people,
not people to serve the law.

What is one way
that I may be running the risk
of putting "law" or "things"
ahead of people in my everyday dealings?

*Better to be kind at home
than to burn incense in a distant place.*
CHINESE PROVERB

WEDNESDAY
Ordinary Time
Week 2

*[A man with a paralyzed hand
entered the synagogue.]
Some people were there
who wanted to accuse Jesus of doing wrong;
so they watched him closely to see whether
he would cure the man on the Sabbath.*

MARK 3:2

Old people in a European town
used to bless themselves as they passed
a certain spot at a wall. They could
give no reason why they did this,
other than their elders used to do it.
One day workers were cleaning the wall.
As they scraped, they found a mural
of Mary and the child Jesus.
People had once blessed themselves
for a reason. Now they did it blindly.
It was simply a ritual they performed.
Some ancient Jews did this also.
Their religion had fossilized into ritual.
Jesus challenged this idea of religion.

How do I try to keep my religion
from becoming simply a ritual—
rather than an act of love?

*In prayer it is better to have
a heart without words
than words without a heart.*

JOHN BUNYAN

THURSDAY
Ordinary Time
Week 2 _____

The sick kept pushing their way to [Jesus]
in order to touch him.
And whenever the people
who had evil spirits in them saw him,
they would fall down before him
and scream, "You are the Son of God!"
Jesus sternly ordered the evil spirits
not to tell anyone who he was.

MARK 3:10–12

Egyptians called kings "sons of god."
Romans called emperors "sons of god."
Jews called good people "sons of God."
So why did Jesus silence evil spirits
when they called him the "Son of God"?
It was because the evil spirits
used the title in a *literal* sense,
not in a *figurative* sense.
Thus Jesus silences them because
he knows that people aren't yet ready
for this incredible revelation.
They must be educated to it gradually.

If Jesus appeared to me and offered
to answer any questions I asked him,
what might one of my questions be?

I had a thousand questions to ask God;
but when I met God, they all fled
and didn't seem to matter.

CHRISTOPHER MORLEY

FRIDAY
Ordinary Time
Week 2

*Jesus went up a hill
and called to himself the men he wanted.
They came to him, and he chose twelve,
whom he named apostles.*

MARK 3:13–14

Jesus called James and John *boanerges,*
which may be translated "hotheads."
They were hardly the kind of persons
you'd expect to lead people to holiness.
Matthew was a tax collector,
someone who collaborated with Rome.
You'd hardly expect him to be the kind
of person to lead people to holiness.
Simon was a member of the Zealot party,
a group of terrorists, bent upon
liquidating every Roman soldier.
You'd hardly expect him to be the kind
of person to lead others to holiness.
Jesus saw beyond what people were
to what they were capable of being.

To what extent do I try to see
beyond people—from what they are
to what they are capable of being?
Who is one person, especially,
who needs me to do this?

*The flowers of all the tomorrows
are in the seeds of today.*

CHINESE PROVERB

SATURDAY
Ordinary Time
Week 2 _____

Such a large crowd gathered
that Jesus and his disciples
had no time to eat.
When his family heard about it,
they set out to take charge of him,
because people were saying,
"He's gone mad!"   MARK 3:20-21

J. D. Salinger wrote a story called "Teddy."
It's about a young person
who finds it hard to live
a spiritual life in today's world.
Teddy says:
"I mean it's very hard to meditate
and live a spiritual life in America.
People think you're a freak. . . .
My father thinks I'm a freak, in a way.
And my mother—
well, she doesn't think it's good for me
to think about God all the time."
Jesus had the same problem
with many of his friends and relatives.

How do people react to my efforts
to live a spiritual life in today's world?

Whenever you find yourself
on the side of the majority,
it is time to pause and reflect.
                    MARK TWAIN

SUNDAY
Ordinary Time
Week 3

*As Jesus walked
along the shore of Lake Galilee,
he saw two brothers who were fishermen,
Simon (called Peter)
and his brother Andrew,
catching fish in the lake with a net.
Jesus said to them, "Come with me,
and I will teach you to catch men."
At once they left their nets
and went with him.*   MATTHEW 4:18-20

Psychologist Abraham Maslow
has an interesting response
to the question of why so few people
"leave all" to follow a dream—
or to pursue a noble goal.
He says they are afraid to become
what they are capable of being.
They thrill at the possiblility,
but they also shudder at it.

How do I respond to the thought
of stepping out in faith
and following Jesus more closely?
How do I react to the idea
of embarking upon a noble goal with Jesus?

*What I am is God's gift to me.
What I become is my gift back to God.*
ANONYMOUS

MONDAY
Ordinary Time
Week 3 _____

[When people credited Jesus' miracles
to the evil spirit, not the Holy Spirit,
Jesus said,] "People can be forgiven
all their sins. . . .
But whoever says evil things
against the Holy Spirit
will never be forgiven,
because he has committed an eternal sin."

MARK 3:28–29

An African boy and some Western adults
survived a plane crash in a jungle.
The boy said he knew the way out,
but the adults ignored him.
They went their own way and perished.
Meanwhile, the African boy survived.
This story gives us a possible insight
into the sin against the Holy Spirit.
It is to ignore
the presence of the Spirit in Jesus.
It is to credit to the evil spirit
what belongs only to the Holy Spirit.

How might I open my heart more fully
to the action of the Spirit in my life?

If Jesus had been indicted in a modern court,
he would have been examined by two doctors,
found to be obsessed by a delusion
and sent to an asylum.

GEORGE BERNARD SHAW

[Jesus said,] "Who is my mother?
Who are my brothers? . . .
Whoever does what God wants . . .
is my brother, my sister, my mother."

MARK 3:33, 35

Kathryn Koob was one of 52 Americans
held hostage by Iran for 444 days
in the 1980s. A source of strength
in dealing with the difficult situation
was found in these words of an old hymn:
"Have thine own way, Lord!
Have thine own way!
Thou are the potter; I am the clay.
Mold me and make me after thy will."
These words gave Kathryn
not only great peace of mind
but also great strength
to resign herself completely to
whatever was God's will in the matter.

Kathryn's readiness to accept God's will
invites me to recall a time
when I had to make a special effort
to resign myself to God's will.

God, give me the serenity to accept
what I can't change,
the courage to change what I can,
and the wisdom to know the difference.

REINHOLD NIEBUHR (slightly adapted)

WEDNESDAY
Ordinary Time
Week 3 _____

[Jesus compared seeds to people.
Seeds that fall among thorns
sprout up, but soon the thorns
choke the tiny plants to death.
These seeds are like people]
"who hear the message,
but the worries about this life . . .
crowd in and choke the message,
and they don't bear fruit."

MARK 4:18-19

A high school girl said to her teacher:
"When we were talking about the
Parable of the Sower, I got the feeling
that Jesus was talking right to me.
Some time ago, my counselor and I
had a talk and I made several resolutions.
Then, yesterday, it hit me.
I hadn't kept one of those resolutions.
I had let all of them get lost
in my worries about school and life."

To what extent am I like the girl—
and the seeds that fell among thorns?
To what extent am I letting the worries
of life choke God's word in my heart?

The more faithfully you listen
to the word within you, the better you hear
what is sounding outside of you.

GEORGE DANA BOARDMAN

[One day Jesus startled people, saying,]
"The person who has something
will be given more . . .
[while the person who has little]
will have taken from him
even the little he has."

MARK 4:25

A monk spent his whole life
sitting and meditating in a dark cave.
His disciples brought him
a few grains of wheat to eat
and a few drops of water to drink.
Because the monk
ceased to use his eyes and his feet,
he lost his ability to see and to walk.

Spiritual ability is like physical ability.
The more we use it, the better it gets.
The less we use it, the weaker it gets.
If we stop using it altogether,
we soon lose what little we had.
To what extent might I be in danger
of losing my spiritual powers,
like the ability to trust and love,
because of lack of use?

Christianity has not been tried
and found wanting.
It hasn't been tried.

GILBERT K. CHESTERTON (slightly adapted)

FRIDAY
Ordinary Time
Week 3 _____

[Jesus said,
"A person] takes a mustard seed,
the smallest seed in the world,
and plants it in the ground.
After a while it grows up
and becomes the biggest of all plants."

MARK 4:31-32

Amado Nervo wrote a poem
that relates to Jesus' parable.
A portion of it reads:
"I'm only a spark,
Make me a fire.
I'm only a string,
Make me a lyre.
I'm only an ant-hill,
Make me a mountain.
I'm only a drop,
Make me a fountain."

How convinced am I
that if Jesus can take a tiny seed
and turn it into a great plant,
he can also take my tiny talent
and turn it into something great
for the Kingdom of God?

[God] chose
what the world considers weak . . .
to shame the powerful.

1 CORINTHIANS 1:27

SATURDAY
Ordinary Time
Week 3

[Jesus and his disciples were at sea.]
"Suddenly a strong wind blew up. . . .
[The disciples grew terribly afraid.]
Jesus stood up and commanded the wind,
"Be quiet!" and he said to the waves,
"Be still!" The wind died down,
and there was a great calm.

MARK 4:37, 39

Helen Keller was blind, deaf, and dumb.
One day, as a child, she climbed a tree.
Suddenly a storm blew up and began
to bend the tree violently. Helen said:
"Just as I was thinking
that the tree and I should fall together
my teacher seized my hand
and helped me down.
I clung to her, trembling with joy."
This story illustrates the kind of fear
that gripped the disciples
during the storm on the Sea of Galilee.
It also helps us to appreciate
their joy and peace when Jesus stilled it.

How do I handle the emotional
and spiritual storms in my life?
How do I help others in their storms?

Lord of the wind and the waves,
stand up and calm our storms
when all seems lost.

SUNDAY
Ordinary Time
Week 4 _____

[Jesus said,] "Happy are those
who know they are spiritually poor;
the Kingdom of heaven belongs to them!"

MATTHEW 5:3

A Hindu parable concerns two friends:
a mud pie and a dry leaf.
One day, they decide to pilgrimage
to the holy city of Benares.
Knowing the wind and the rain
will be their enemies on the pilgrimage,
they devise a plan for protection.
When the wind blows,
the mud pie will sit on the dry leaf;
and when the rain pours, the leaf
will sit on the mud pie to keep it dry.
The plan worked fine, until one day
the wind blew and the rain poured
at the same time. The result?
The leaf blew away and
the mud pie dissolved into nothingness.

To be "poor in spirit" means to realize
that we cannot go through life alone.
There will be times when even our friends
can't help us. We will need God.

[Jesus said,] "I am the vine,
and you are the branches. . . .
You can do nothing without me."

JOHN 15:5

*[After driving an evil spirit out of a man,
Jesus told him,] "Go back home
to your family and tell them
how much the Lord has done for you
and how kind he has been to you."
So the man left. . . .
And all who heard it were amazed.*

MARK 5:19-20

Young Ruddell Norris was aware
that every Christian is called by baptism
to spread the good news of the Gospel.
His problem was that he was shy.
How could he spread
the good news of the Gospel?
Ruddell's solution was ingenious.
He spent a certain percentage
of his allowance on religious pamphlets
and placed them in hospital lobbies
and other appropriate places.
One day he overheard someone saying,
"My introduction to the Church
came through a pamphlet that I found
in a hospital lobby."

What is one concrete thing I might do
to help spread the message of Jesus?

*When Jesus teaches me to sing his song,
how can I keep from singing it?*

ANONYMOUS

TUESDAY
Ordinary Time
Week 4 _____

[A woman had been ill for twelve years.
One day she touched Jesus,
believing that he would cure her.]
Jesus said to her, "My daughter,
your faith has made you well.
Go in peace, and be healed."

MARK 5:34

Years ago, Joseph Lewis,
head of the Freethinkers of America,
said over station WMIE in Miami,
"If I had the power
that the Bible says that Jesus had,
I would not cure one person of blindness,
I would make blindness impossible;
I would not cure one person of leprosy,
I would abolish leprosy."

Why didn't Jesus abolish ills,
like blindness and leprosy?
How might Jesus' response to the woman
in today's gospel suggest one answer?

How often we look upon God
as our last and feeblest resource.
We go to God because we have
nowhere else to go. And then we learn
that the storms of life have driven us
not upon the rocks
but into the desired haven.

GEORGE MACDONALD

—————————— SPECIAL NOTE

Starting with Wednesday of the fourth week of Ordinary Time, the *Lectionary* readings vary from year to year, depending on when Ash Wednesday (start of Lent) falls in that year.

The following table shows the date on which Ash Wednesday falls in the years ahead. Locate the current year and, on the date indicated, turn to page 67 (Ash Wednesday) and begin there.

1992	March 4
1993	February 24
1994	February 16
1995	March 1
1996	February 21
1997	February 12
1998	February 25
1999	February 17
2000	March 8
2001	February 28
2002	February 13
2003	March 5
2004	February 25
2005	February 9
2006	March 1
2007	February 21
2008	February 6
2009	February 25
2010	February 17

WEDNESDAY
Ordinary Time
Week 4

[Some people from Jesus' home town
rejected him, saying,]
"Isn't he the carpenter,
the son of Mary?"...
[Jesus] was not able
to perform any miracles there ...
because the people did not have faith.

MARK 6:3, 5-6

Father Paride Taban returned to Sudan
after being ordained a priest in Uganda.
At first, his people rejected him.
"You are a priest?" they said.
"We find that hard to believe.
You are black like us.
You are a member of the Madi tribe.
How can you be a priest of God,
like the white missionaries?"
Paride responded with understanding.
Two years later those who rejected him
accepted Paride with profound affection.

The rejections of Jesus and Paride
invite me to ask:
How do I handle rejection,
especially by those I love?

To maintain a well-balanced perspective,
the person who has a dog to worship him
should also have a cat to ignore him.

AUTHOR UNKNOWN

THURSDAY
Ordinary Time
Week 4

*[Jesus sent his disciples out to preach,
saying,] "Don't take anything with you . . .
no bread . . . no money. . . ."
He also told them,
"Wherever you are welcomed, stay."*

MARK 6:8, 10

Seminarian Richard Roos wanted to know
how it felt to be without food or money.
One Lent he begged and walked 800 miles
from San Diego to San Francisco. He wrote:
"Every afternoon at two or three o'clock
I'd begin to feel a growing anxiety
about where I would wind up
spending the night. . . . And of course,
I felt the powerlessness of poverty.
When you go to a door . . .
and ask for food and lodging . . .
you find yourself feeling very humble.
You've just handed over the whole deck
to the other person, and it's their deal.
You have no rights or power."
NATIONAL JESUIT NEWS

Why did Jesus tell his disciples
to take no food or money?
Would he still tell them that today?

*Once a guy starts wearing silk pajamas,
it's hard to get up early.*

JOCKEY EDDIE ARCARO

FRIDAY
Ordinary Time
Week 4 _____

[After Herod arrested John the Baptist,]
he had him tied up and put in prison.
Herod did this because of Herodias,
whom he had married, even though
she was the wife of his brother Philip.
John the Baptist kept telling Herod,
"It isn't right for you
to marry your brother's wife!"

MARK 6:17-18

The naturalist Henry David Thoreau
went to jail rather than pay a poll tax
to support the Mexican War.
Like many, he saw the war as a move
to expand slave-holding territories.
He could not support a government
that supported slavery.
Ralph Waldo Emerson, who hated slavery too,
visited him in jail and said,
"Henry, why are you here?" Thoreau replied,
"Waldo, why are you *not* here?"

John the Baptist and Henry David Thoreau
paid a price for opposing evil.
When did I pay a price for opposing evil?
What can I do when the price is high?

The only thing necessary
for the triumph of evil
is for good people to do nothing.

EDMUND BURKE (slightly adapted)

[One day Jesus said to his disciples,]
"Let us go off by ourselves to some place
where we will be alone and
you can rest a while." So they started out
in a boat by themselves to a lonely place.

MARK 6:31-32

Years ago, Dr. W. R. Luxton wrote:
"I cannot overstate the importance
of the habit of quiet meditation
for health of body, mind, and spirit.
Modern man's life is grossly abnormal. . . .
We need to explore our lives . . .
quietly and unhurried in his presence."

Since I started setting aside time
for quiet prayer and reflection,
how has the experience affected me?

[We] must get away now and then
to experience loneliness. Only those
who learn how to live with loneliness
can come to know themselves and life.
I go out there and walk
and look at the trees and sky.
I listen to the sounds of loneliness.
I sit on a rock . . . and say to myself,
"Who are you, Sandburg?
Where have you been,
and where are you going?"

CARL SANDBURG

SUNDAY
Ordinary Time
Week 5 _____

[Jesus said,]
"You are like light for the whole world.
A city built on a hill cannot be hid. . . .
In the same way
your light must shine before people,
so that they will see the good things
you do and praise your Father in heaven."

MATTHEW 5:14, 16

"Nineteen-year-old Nancy Powell
was killed in a car crash near Houston.
Her tragic death brought an outpouring
of emotion from all who knew her.
One young man said of her:
'Her purity, freshness, enthusiasm,
and most of all her ability to love,
bathed all of us who were around her.
She was truly a joy.
Nancy's essence was that she saw people
for what they really were, but loved them
as if they were at their best.
Her special kind of love
will be a motivator throughout my life.' "
ALBERT CYLWICKI

To what extent
could this same thing be said about me?

Lighthouses blow no horns;
they only shine.
DWIGHT L. MOODY

Everywhere Jesus went . . . .
people would take their sick . . . .
and beg him
to let the sick at least touch
the edge of his cloak.
And all who touched it were made well.

MARK 6:56

On Christmas of 1980,
three clergymen were allowed to meet
with 52 Americans held hostage in Iran.
They conducted services for them
and gave them messages from home.
One clergyman told hostage Barry Rosen,
"I saw your wife, Barbara,
and your son, Alexander, in New York.
Alexander asked me to give you this."
Then he placed a kiss on Barry's cheek.
Barry could hardly fight back the tears.

Touch communicates in a powerful way.
Small wonder people touched Jesus.
Small wonder they were healed
when they touched him.
To what extent do I affirm people,
especially members of my own family,
by a hug or a kiss?

Give people not only your care,
but also your heart.

MOTHER TERESA

TUESDAY
Ordinary Time
Week 5 _____

[Jesus rebuked some Pharisees, saying,]
"How right Isaiah was
when he prophesied about you! . . .
'These people . . . teach man-made rules
as though they were my laws!' "

MARK 7:6-7

William Barclay tells
how a jailed rabbi nearly died of thirst,
because he used his small daily ration
of water for ritual handwashing,
rather than for drinking.
Strict observance of external practices
was both a strength and a weakness
for many Jews, especially the Pharisees.
It made them a strong, religious people.
But it also turned some of them
into religious formalists, who placed
more importance on external rituals
than on attitudes of the heart,
like love, service, and compassion.

When it comes to worship, do I sometimes
place more importance on external things
than on internal attitudes of the heart?

The test of true worship is how far
it makes us more sensitive
to the "beyond in our midst," to the Christ
in the hungry, the naked, the homeless.

JOHN ROBINSON in *Honest To God*

[Jesus said,] "There is nothing
that goes into a person from the outside
which can make him ritually unclean. . . .
It is what comes out of a person
that makes him unclean.
For from the inside,
from a person's heart, come the evil ideas
which lead him to do immoral things."

MARK 7:15, 20-21

The Second Book of Maccabees tells
how Syria conquered Israel in 170 B.C.
and tried to wipe out the Jewish faith.
For example,
seven children were tortured and killed,
while their mother looked on,
because they wouldn't eat unclean food.
Stories like this inspired Jews
to respect ancient traditions.
Unfortunately, some traditionalists
began to put more stress on unclean food
than on an unclean heart.
It was this kind of religious error
that Jesus had to correct.

What external rituals do I find helpful
in my own religious worship?

I rarely kneel because I feel reverent,
but because I want to feel reverent.

AUTHOR UNKNOWN

THURSDAY
Ordinary Time
Week 5 _____

*[A Gentile woman asked Jesus to heal
her child. Jesus tested her, saying,]*
*"It isn't right to take the children's food
and throw it to the dogs."*
*"Sir," she answered, "even the dogs . . .
eat the children's leftovers!"*
[Then Jesus healed her child.]

MARK 7:27-28

A little girl went to a friend's home
for supper. When everyone was seated,
she bowed her head, waiting for grace.
When no one prayed, she said,
"You're like my dog, you just start in."
Jews felt the same way about Gentiles.
They were insensitive to God.
The Greek word Jesus used for "dog"
refers to a pet dog, not a street dog.
Jesus used the word in a playful way,
as parents use the word *rascal* playfully,
saying to a child, "You little rascal!"
The woman's reply suggests as much.

How do I approach Jesus for help—
confidently, even aggressively,
as did the Gentile woman? Why?

*If you knock
long enough and loud enough . . .
you are sure to wake up somebody.*
HENRY WADSWORTH LONGFELLOW

FRIDAY
Ordinary Time
Week 5

Some people brought [Jesus] a man
who was deaf and could hardly speak. . . .
Jesus looked up to heaven,
gave a deep groan, and said to the man,
"Ephphatha," which means, "Open up!"
At once the man was able to hear . . .
and he began to talk without any trouble.

MARK 7:32, 34-35

Because of her deafness, Helen Keller
never learned to speak until Miss Fuller,
a speech teacher, paved the way.
She put Helen's hand to her own face
to let Helen feel the positions of her lips
and tongue when she spoke to Helen.
Helen then tried to duplicate them.
After long practice, Helen learned to talk.
Her joy was unbounded. She wrote later:
"I used to repeat ecstatically,
'I am not dumb now.' "
This is how the dumb man in the Gospel
must have felt when Jesus healed him.

How appreciative am I of my gifts
of hearing, speech, and sight?
Which of these gifts
do I have a tendency to misuse? How?

I wept because I had no shoes,
until I saw someone who had no feet.

ANCIENT PERSIAN SAYING

SATURDAY
Ordinary Time
Week 5 _____

[One day Jesus took seven loaves,]
gave thanks to God, broke them,
and gave them . . . to the crowd. . . .
Everybody ate and had enough—
there were about four thousand people.
MARK 8:6, 8

Saint Mark avoids repetition.
Yet, he tells a similar story earlier
(MARK 6:38-44). Why the repetition here?
Study shows it isn't a repetition.
Jesus himself refers to both "feedings"
(MARK 8:19-21).
How are the two stories different, then?
The first involved only Jews;
the second included Gentiles.
Scholars agree Gentiles were present
because of the location (MARK 7:31).
Thus, the second "feeding" foreshadows
the day when Jews and Gentiles
will break bread together
as the one family of God (ACTS 10).

Why is it not always easy
to "break bread" as one family of God?

In Christ there is no East or West,
In him no South or North,
But one great fellowship of love
throughout the whole wide earth.
OLD HYMN

SUNDAY
Ordinary Time
Week 6

*[Jesus gave this example to illustrate
that our worship on Sunday
should reflect what we seek to be
during the week. He said,]*
*"If you are about to offer
your gift to God at the altar
and there you remember that your brother
[or sister] has something against you,
leave your gift . . . and make peace . . .
then come back and offer your gift."*

MATTHEW 5:23-24

In his autobiography, Mahatma Gandhi
tells how in his student days
in South Africa he was drawn to Jesus.
One Sunday, Gandhi writes,
he went to a Christian church.
He was stopped at the entrance and told
that if he desired to attend services,
he was welcome to do so in a church
reserved for black people.
Gandhi did not pursue the matter further.

What is one way that my daily behavior
might better reflect what I profess
on Sunday: we are one family under God?

*People look at us the rest of the week
to see what we really meant
by our worship together on Sunday.*

ANONYMOUS

MONDAY
Ordinary Time
Week 6 _____

*Some Pharisees came to Jesus
and started to argue with him.
They wanted to trap him.*

MARK 8:11

An old story concerns
a boy and his grandfather
leading a donkey down a road.
Someone laughed at them for being stupid
and not riding the donkey.
So the grandfather rode the donkey
until someone criticized him
for making the boy walk.
Then the boy rode the donkey
until someone criticized him
for lacking respect for elders.
Finally, both rode the donkey
until someone criticized them
for being cruel to animals.

The moral of the story is fairly clear.
Jesus faced similar problems
with similar people in his day.
And 2,000 years haven't changed things.
How do I respond to people who are
consistently negative about everything?

*Pessimists complain about the wind.
Optimists hope it will change.
Realists adjust the sails.*

WILLIAM ARTHUR WARD (slightly adapted)

TUESDAY
Ordinary Time
Week 6

The disciples
had forgotten to bring enough bread
and had only one loaf with them. . . .
[Jesus saw their concern and said,]
"Why are you discussing
about not having any bread?
Don't you know or understand yet?"

MARK 8:14, 17

Years ago, a seminarian went on
a month-long pilgrimage, taking no money.
He wanted to feel what it was like
to have to beg for food and lodging
and to put all his trust in God.
"Many a night," he said, "I experienced
near panic at not yet having found
a place to stay or a meal to eat."

The disciples experienced similar panic
in today's gospel reading, even though
they had seen Jesus feed big crowds.
Jesus chided them, saying in effect,
"Where's your trust in my care
about your needs and concerns?"

How much trust do I have in Jesus' care
about my needs and concerns?

The more we depend on God,
the more dependable we find God is.

CLIFF RICHARDS

WEDNESDAY
Ordinary Time
Week 6 _____

[Jesus placed his hands on a blind man.
The man saw, but not clearly.]
Jesus again placed his hands
on the man's eyes.
This time the man looked intently,
his eyesight returned, and
he saw everything clearly.

MARK 8:25

Patients who go to a doctor
for treatment of a physical ailment
must often return again and again
before they are healed.
Isn't it strange that we think
a few sessions of prayer should suffice
to heal us of a spiritual ailment?
Today's gospel shows that even Jesus
had to repeat his efforts to heal a man.
Recall also that Jesus repeated over
and over the same prayer for strength
in the Garden of Gethsemane.

How persevering am I
in my prayer and my efforts to be healed
of a spiritual ailment that causes me
to stumble and fall often?

A little girl was asked
how she learned to skate.
She replied,
"Oh, by getting up every time I fell."

[One day Jesus asked his disciples,]
"Who do people say I am?"
[After listening to their answers,
he said,] "What about you? . . .
Who do you say I am?"
Peter answered, "You are the Messiah."

MARK 8:27, 29

Two children, Sue and Tim,
were watching a scorpion.
Sue said, "A scorpion stung me once."
"How badly did it hurt?" asked Tim.
Sue thought a minute.
Then she pinched her arm until it hurt
the way she remembered the sting.
Then she pinched Tim the same way.
Tim said, "That wasn't bad."
Sue shrugged and said,
"Well, I can't feel a sting for you,
but that's about how much it hurt me."

Some things I can't do for another person:
feel a sting, view a sunset,
profess faith in Jesus.
This raises a question: What might I do
to motivate others, especially children,
to do these things for themselves?

An ounce of practice
is worth a pound of preaching.

JOHN RAY

FRIDAY
Ordinary Time
Week 6 _____

[One day Jesus asked a crowd,]
"Does a person gain anything
if he wins the whole world
but loses his life?"   MARK 8:36

In 1923 a high-level meeting was held
in Chicago's old Edgewater Beach Hotel.
Nine of the most powerful people
in the United States were there.
They included the presidents of
the nation's largest steel company,
the nation's largest gas company,
the nation's largest utility company.
Twenty-five years later,
where were these powerful tycoons?
Three had died penniless, three had
committed suicide, two were in prison,
and one had gone insane.

The fates of these business people
illustrate Jesus' point in today's gospel.
They also invite me to ask myself:
To what extent could I be in danger
of making the same mistake they did?

Give us clear vision that we may know
where to stand and for what to stand,
because unless we stand for something,
we shall fall for anything.

                              PETER MARSHALL

SATURDAY
Ordinary Time
Week 6

[Jesus was with three disciples.
Suddenly a cloud appeared,
and a voice came from it, saying,]
"This is my own dear Son—listen to him!"

MARK 9:7

A *Peanuts* cartoon shows Schroeder
with a record of Brahm's Fourth Symphony.
"Whataya going to do with it?" asks Lucy.
"Listen to it," says Schroeder.
"You mean dance to it or sing along with it
or tap your feet to it?" asks Lucy.
"No, just listen to it," says Schroeder.
"Dumbest thing I ever heard," says Lucy.

We find it hard to listen.
We feel we must be "doing" something.
But the voice from the cloud didn't say,
"This is my Son, love him," or
"This is my Son, reach out to him," or
"This is my Son, worship him."
The voice from the cloud said,
"This is my Son, listen to him!"
This raises a question:
How do I go about listening to Jesus?

A wise old owl sat on an oak,
The more he saw the less he spoke;
The less he spoke the more he heard;
Why aren't we like that wise old bird?

EDWARD HERSEY RICHARDS

SUNDAY
Ordinary Time
Week 7 _____

*"Love your enemies
and pray for those who persecute you."*

MATTHEW 5:44

Corrie ten Boom was a survivor
of a Nazi concentration camp.
After the war she toured Europe
giving talks, urging rival nations
to forgive one another.
One night, after a talk in Munich,
a man came up and extended his hand
in a gesture of reconciliation.
He was one of the most hated guards
of the camp she'd been in.
She couldn't take his hand. She prayed,
"Jesus, help me! I can't forgive him!"
Instantly, some higher power helped her
to take his hand in forgiveness.
That night Corrie learned a great truth.
The same Jesus who taught us to love
our enemies empowers us to do it.
All we need do is to ask for the power.

When was the last time I prayed for
a person who had hurt me? Pick out
such a person now and pray for him or her.

*Who has not forgiven an enemy
has not yet tasted
one of the most sublime enjoyments of life.*

JOHN KASPAR LAVATER

*[A man begged Jesus to heal his son,
saying,] "Help us, if you possibly can!"
"Yes," said Jesus, "if you yourself can!
Everything is possible for the person
who has faith."* MARK 9:22-23

Lew Miller
went from 190 pounds to 90 pounds.
He began to despair of recovery.
Then he remembered Jesus' words:
"Everything is possible for the person
who has faith."
And so Lew began to pray for healing,
meditating on how it might take place.
He says: "I visualized my body
coming alive with life-giving spirit. . . .
I saw myself walking . . . running."
To the amazement of doctors,
Lew slowly regained complete health.

Asked if he believed in a higher power,
Dr. Carl Jung said:
"I could not say I believe. I know!
I have had the experience of being gripped
by something stronger than myself,
something people call God."

*Strong beliefs win strong people,
and make them stronger.*
WALTER BAGEHOT

TUESDAY
Ordinary Time
Week 7 _____

[Jesus heard his disciples arguing
about who was the greatest.]
Jesus sat down . . . and said to them,
"Whoever wants to be first
must place himself last of all
and be the servant of all."

MARK 9:35

The former American Communist
Whittaker Chambers
wrote a best-seller entitled *Witness*.
In it he describes a hero of his youth,
a Communist-party leader in Poland,
named Felix Djerkinsky.
While in prison for his political views,
Felix insisted on doing the dirtiest jobs,
like cleaning the public toilets.
He believed that a true leader
should be willing to do
whatever he asks others to do.

Felix's ideas about leadership
and Jesus' words
about those who aspire to be first,
invite me to ask myself:
To what extent do I agree with them?
To what extent do I follow them?

You can't lead anyone any further
than you have gone yourself.

GENE MAUCH

WEDNESDAY
Ordinary Time
Week 7

[One day a disciple told Jesus,]
"Teacher, we saw a man who was
driving out demons in your name,
and we told him to stop,
because he doesn't belong to our group."
"Do not try to stop him,"
Jesus told them. . . .
"For whoever is not against us is for us."

MARK 9:38-40

Ancients believed demons caused
certain physical and mental illnesses.
One way they combated these illnesses
was to invoke a more powerful spirit
to expel the demon causing the illness.
This is what
the disciple in today's reading refers to.
When Jesus says,
"Whoever is not against us is for us,"
he is saying in effect
that so long as evil is destroyed,
it makes no difference who destroys it.
The result is the same: good triumphs.

How much am I willing to sacrifice
to defeat evil, even if I should get
little or no recognition for it?

You're either a part of the solution
or a part of the problem.

ELDRIDGE CLEAVER

THURSDAY
Ordinary Time
Week 7 _____

[Jesus shocked his listeners, saying,]
"If your foot
makes you lose your faith, cut it off!
It is better for you to enter life
without a foot than to keep both feet
and be thrown into hell."

MARK 9:45

Jesus' point is this:
Root out from your life whatever threatens
your relationship with God.
Spare no pain to root it out.
William Barclay puts it this way:
"It might seem like
cutting out part of our own body,
but if we are to know real life,
real happiness, real peace, it must go."

What is one thing, right now,
that could be a threat
to my relationship with God?
Speak to God about it.

There are three attitudes toward giving:
grudge giving,
duty giving,
and thanks giving.
Grudge giving says, "I hate to";
duty giving says, "I ought to";
thanks giving says, "I want to."

ROBERT RODENMAYER (slightly adapted)

[Jesus said,]
" 'God made them male and female,'
as the scripture says.
'And for this reason
a man will leave his father and mother and
unite with his wife,
and the two will become one.'
So they are no longer two, but one."

MARK 10:6-8

An old story concerns a couple
who knocked at the door of a house.
A voice from within said, "Who is it?"
The young man said, "It is I.
I've come to ask to marry your daughter."
The voice from within said,
"You're not ready; come back in a year."
A year later the couple returned
and knocked again at the door.
The voice from within said, "Who is it?"
The youth said, "It is your daughter and I.
We've come to ask your permission to marry."
The voice said, "Please come in."

When did I feel the greatest oneness
with my spouse or another person?

Love is the only force
that can make things one
without destroying them.
TEILHARD DE CHARDIN

SATURDAY
Ordinary Time
Week 7 _____

Some people
brought children to Jesus. . . .
[Jesus] took the children in his arms,
placed his hands on each of them,
and blessed them.

MARK 10:13, 16

A woman social worker and some boys
attended a talk by Bill Russell,
the great basketball superstar.
After the talk, she asked Bill
to come over and say
a few encouraging words to the boys.
Bill was familiar with boys like these;
he had grown up with them.
So he responded to her request.
Referring to the episode later, he said:
"I told those kids I wasn't going
to give them the same old crap
that they'd heard so often. . . .
And then I shook hands with them,
because I wanted them to know
that I cared about them enough
to touch them."

How do I show people I care about them?

I don't think I ever hugged my father. . . .
I needed emotional love and support.
I never ever got that.

MARK CHAPMAN, convicted killer

SUNDAY
Ordinary Time
Week 8

[Jesus said,]
"No one can be a slave of two masters;
he will hate one and love the other;
he will be loyal to one
and despise the other.
You cannot serve both God and money."

MATTHEW 6:24

A woman was about to take a shower.
She had one foot in the shower
and the other foot on the bathroom rug.
As she stood in this awkward position,
she thought to herself,
"This is a good picture of my life."
She had long wanted to commit her life
to God, but she could never quite do it.
She kept one foot in and one foot out.
Now the time had come to decide.
She paused for a long time.
Then, taking a deep breath, she said aloud,
"I choose you, Lord!"
With that, she stepped into the shower.
It was like being baptized.

Is there an area
in my relationship with the Lord
where I am failing to be decisive,
keeping one foot in and one foot out?

Not to decide is to decide.
HARVEY COX

MONDAY
Ordinary Time
Week 8 _____

*[One day Jesus invited a man to sell
all his possessions and follow him.]*
**When the man heard this,
gloom spread over his face,
and he went away sad,
because he was very rich.**

MARK 10:22

A Peruvian boy found a priceless pearl.
"My worries are over," he thought.
"I'll sell it and never have to work again."
But when the boy tried to sell the pearl,
the buyers put him off.
Later, he was attacked several times.
Now he knew the pearl buyers
wanted to rob him and possibly kill him.
He had to choose
between the pearl and his life.
With the pearl buyers looking on,
he went down to the beach,
took his pearl, and threw it into the sea.

The boy's action contrasts sharply
with the man in today's gospel reading.
It invites me to ask: What kind of hold
do material possessions have on me?

*When wealth is lost, nothing is lost;
when health is lost, something is lost.
When character is lost, all is lost.*

ANONYMOUS

[Jesus said to his disciples,]
"Many who are now first will be last,
and many who are now last
will be first."

MARK 10:31

James M. Barrie wrote a play
about the servant of a wealthy family.
The servant was ordered about
and treated as the lowest of the low.
One day the family took an ocean trip.
A shipwreck ensued
and the family and the servant
ended up on a deserted island.
The family was totally helpless.
The servant alone knew what to do.
Suddenly, the servant's status
changed from that of being last
to that of being first.

The story illustrates
the point Jesus makes in today's reading.
It also challenges me to ask myself:
To what extent
do I tend to judge people
by the world's standards, not by God's?

The Don Quixote of one generation
may live to hear himself called
the savior of society by the next.

JAMES RUSSELL LOWELL

WEDNESDAY
Ordinary Time
Week 8 _____

*[One day Jesus overheard his disciples
arguing about who was the greatest.
He said to them,]*
*"If one of you wants to be great,
he must be the servant of the rest."*

MARK 10:43

Dr. Elisabeth Kubler-Ross
is a former professor of psychiatry
at the University of Chicago.
She interviewed hundreds of people
involved in near-death experiences.
Consistently, they reported
a kind of instant replay of their lives.
It was like seeing a rapid-fire movie
of everything they had ever said or done.
"When you come to this point,"
says Dr. Kubler-Ross,
"you see there are only two things
that are relevant:
the service you rendered to others
and love.
All those things we think are important,
like fame, money, prestige, and power,
are insignificant."

How operative
are service and love in my life?

Let us be paths to be used and forgotten.
PAUL CLAUDEL

*[A blind person
called out to Jesus in a loud voice,]*
"Son of David, have mercy on me!"
[Jesus healed the person, saying,]
"Go, . . . your faith has made you well."

MARK 10:48, 52

A nun asked little Mary, "Who made you?"
Mary looked puzzled for a minute.
Then she said, "God made part of me."
Now the nun looked puzzled, saying,
"Did you say that God made *part* of you?"
"Yes," said Mary,
"God made me tiny; but the rest—
God and I did that together."

My Christian life is something like that.
It is a joint effort between God and me.
Without my faith, God can do nothing.
With it, we can do anything together.
This raises a question:
How firmly do I believe
that if I put faith in Jesus,
he can do anything through me,
in spite of my flaws?

*It is never a question with any of us
of faith or no faith;
the question always is,
"In what or in whom do I put my faith?"*

ANONYMOUS

FRIDAY
Ordinary Time
Week 8 _____

[One day Jesus said to his disciples,]
"Have faith in God. . . .
When you pray and ask for something,
believe . . . , and you
will be given whatever you ask for."

MARK 11:22, 24

Thirteen-year-old Anne Frank and
her Jewish family evaded the Nazis
for two years before being caught
during World War II.
She kept a diary of the ordeal.
After the war
her diary was found and published.
One entry reads:
"I still believe
that people are really good at heart. . . .
If I look into the heavens
I think that it will all come out right
and that peace and tranquility
will return again."
Anne died in a concentration camp.

How deeply do I have faith and hope
in people and in the future? Why?

When you say
a situation or person is hopeless,
you are slamming the door
in the face of God.

CHARLES L. ALLEN

SATURDAY
Ordinary Time
Week 8

[Jesus asked some people,]
"Where did John's right to baptize come from:
was it from God or from man?"
[To avoid the consequences
of an honest answer, they responded,]
"We don't know."

MARK 11:30, 33

Years ago a cigarette company
ran an extensive advertising campaign.
The image they chose to spearhead it
was a person with a black eye
smoking a cigarette.
Beneath the picture of the person
were the words:
"I'd rather fight than switch."
There were a lot of people
in Jesus' time like that.
They closed their eyes and their ears
to everything that Jesus did and said.
They would "rather fight than switch."
They were not open to truth.

How open am I to truth and change?
When does firmness in one's position
become obstinacy or pigheadedness?

I am firm.
You are obstinate.
He is a pigheaded fool.
KATHARINE WHITEHORN

SUNDAY
Ordinary Time
Week 9 _____

[Jesus said to the people,]
"Anyone who hears these words of mine
and does not obey them
is like a foolish man
who built his house on sand.
The rain poured down,
the rivers flooded over,
the wind blew hard against that house,
and it fell.
And what a terrible fall that was!"

MATTHEW 7:26-27

A young wife had grown accustomed
to staying in bed while her husband
got up, ate alone, and left for work.
One morning the young husband awoke
to find his wife cooking breakfast.
He wondered, "Why the sudden change?"
Then, he saw on his wife's night table
a copy of the *Reader's Digest,*
open to an article entitled
"Do European Women Make Better Wives?"
His wife was putting into practice
what she had read the night before.

What is one teaching of Jesus
that I find hard to put into practice?

The measure of my belief is this:
the extent to which I put it
into practice.

[Jesus said,]
"Surely you have read this scripture?
'The stone which the builders
rejected as worthless turned out to be
the most important of all.'"

MARK 12:10

In the days of Benjamin Franklin,
horseshoe nails were common.
For instance, you could find them
lying in the dust beside a road.
Most people thought of horseshoe nails
as having little or no value.
To dramatize that just the opposite
is sometimes true,
Franklin wrote the following "poem":
"For want of a nail the shoe was lost.
For want of a shoe the horse was lost.
For want of a horse the rider was lost.
For want of a rider the battle was lost."

Franklin's poem
and Jesus' works invite me to ask:
Do I sometimes treat people around me
as having little or no value?
Who is one such person?
What is one value this person has?

[The Lord said, "People look] at the outward
appearance, but I look at the heart."

1 SAMUEL 16:7

TUESDAY
Ordinary Time
Week 9 _____

*[When Jesus' opponents asked him
if Jews should pay taxes to Rome,
Jesus asked them for a coin, saying,]
"Whose face and name are these?"
"The Emperor's," they answered.
So Jesus said,
"Well, then, pay to the Emperor
what belongs to the Emperor,
and pay to God what belongs to God."
And they were amazed at Jesus.*

MARK 12:16-17

The question raised by Jesus' opponents
was designed to trap him.
If Jesus said they should pay taxes,
he would alienate the people.
If he said they should not pay them,
he would be reported to the Romans.
Jesus exposed their insincerity
by asking them for a Roman coin,
which they gave him.
To have a Roman coin was to admit
a Roman obligation.
The people would have been impressed
that Jesus did not have a Roman coin.

How honest and straightforward am I
in my dealings with other people?

An honest man's the noblest work of God.

ALEXANDER POPE

[Some Sadducees,
who didn't believe in life after death,
tried to trap Jesus by asking him
if a widow who remarries
will have more than one husband in heaven.]
Jesus answered them . . . "You don't know
the Scriptures or God's power.
For when the dead rise to life,
they will be like the angels in heaven
and will not marry."

MARK 12:24-25

The film *The Heart Is a Lonely Hunter*
has a sequence in which a deaf person
asks a girl what music sounds like.
She stands in front of the person
so that he can read her lips.
She also gestures with her hands.
But nothing works.
Finally, they both laugh and give up.

Jesus ran into a similar problem
when he taught people about heaven.
They couldn't imagine what it was like.
How do I envision heaven?

"What no one ever saw or heard,
what no one ever thought could happen,
is the very thing God prepared
for those who love [God]."

1 CORINTHIANS 2:9

THURSDAY
Ordinary Time
Week 9 _____

*[When asked about the commandments,
Jesus said,]
"The most important one is . . .
'Love the Lord your God
with all your heart, with all your soul,
with all your mind,
and with all your strength.'
The second . . . is . . . 'Love your neighbor
as you love yourself.' "*   MARK 12:30-31

An old rabbi asked a disciple,
"How can you tell
when night is over and day has begun?"
The disciple thought a moment
and said, "Could it be
when you see an animal in the distance
and can tell if it is a lamb or a dog?"
"No," answered the rabbi, "think again!"
The disciple did, but to no avail.
The rabbi then said, "It's when
you can look into the face of another
and see that it's your sister or brother.
If you can't see this, it's still night."

What tends to keep me from seeing a brother
or sister in the face of another?

*We must learn to live together as brothers
or perish together as fools.*
                    MARTIN LUTHER KING, JR.

As Jesus was teaching in the Temple,
he asked the question. . . .
"The Holy Spirit inspired David to say:
'The Lord said to my Lord:
Sit here at my right side
until I put your enemies under your feet.'
David himself called him 'Lord';
so how can the Messiah
be David's descendant?"   MARK 12:35-37

Jesus is not denying that the Messiah
is David's descendant.
Rather, he is affirming that the Messiah
transcends human descent.
The Greek word for "Lord"
that Jesus uses is *kurios.*
Greeks reserved this word for *God.*
In other words, Jesus is saying
that the Messiah is
not only the Son of David
but also the Son of God.
He is not just David's descendant
but also David's Lord.

What convinces me most that Jesus
is "Lord" of heaven and earth?

I have a great need for Christ;
I have a great Christ for my need.
          CHARLES SPURGEON

SATURDAY
Ordinary Time
Week 9 _____

[A widow put into the offering box
two copper coins, worth about a penny.
Jesus said to his disciples,]
"This poor widow put more
in the offering box than all the others.
For the others
put in what they had to spare . . .
she gave all she had." MARK 12: 43–44

While walking along a deserted beach,
an Indian holy man found a pearl.
A poor woman saw him pick it up
and asked him to give it to her.
The holy man did so cheerfully.
The woman went off, singing for joy.
She was now wealthy.
A week later, the woman reappeared
and returned the pearl to the man, saying,
"Give me that which is more valuable
than the pearl.
Give me that which enabled you
to give the pearl to me so cheerfully."

What enabled the holy man
to give the pearl away so cheerfully?

What you give in health is gold.
What you give in sickness is silver.
What you give after death is lead.
JEWISH PROVERB

*[Some Pharisees were complaining because
Jesus ate with sinners.]
Jesus heard them and answered,
"People who are well do not need a doctor,
but only those who are sick."*

MATTHEW 9:12

A little girl was playing hide-and-seek
with some friends.
When it came time for her to hide,
she picked out a place and waited.
Five minutes passed, and no one came.
Ten minutes passed, and no one came.
Then the girl learned
her friends had decided to stop playing.
She began to cry because
they weren't playing the game fairly.
An old man heard her and said,
"You have learned a great lesson.
You have learned how God feels."
We were created to seek and find God,
but we aren't playing the game fairly.
While God waits to be found,
we go off and do our own thing.

On a scale of one to ten, how fairly
am I playing the game of life with God?

*If we walk one step toward God,
God will run ten steps toward us.*

ANONYMOUS

MONDAY
Ordinary Time
Week 10 _____

Jesus saw the crowds and went up a hill,
where he sat down.
His disciples gathered around him,
and he began to teach them:
"Happy are those
who know they are spiritually poor;
the Kingdom of heaven belongs to them!
Happy are those who mourn;
God will comfort them!"

MATTHEW 5:1-4

Dr. Tom Dooley
worked among Asia's poor and needy.
One day he told a friend of his love
for the second beatitude:
"Happy are those who mourn."
He explained
that he understood *mourn* to mean
"being extrasensitive to sorrow."
Then, he added,
"If you're extrasensitive to sorrow
and do something to make it lighter—
you can't help but be happy."

How sensitive am I to sorrow
in the lives of people around me?
What might I do to make it lighter?

Love locked in our hearts . . .
is like a letter written and not sent.

JANE LINDSTROM

[Jesus said to his disciples,]
"You are like light for the whole world.
A city built on a hill cannot be hid.
No one lights a lamp
and puts it under a bowl;
instead he puts it on the lampstand,
where it gives light
for everyone in the house.
In the same way
your light must shine before people,
so that they will see the good things you do
and praise your Father in heaven."

MATTHEW 5:14-16

Dr. Albert Schweitzer was voted
the "Man of the Century" for his work
among the poor in Africa.
He said in an interview:
"As I look back upon my youth
I realize how important for me were
the help, understanding and courage . . .
so many people gave me.
These men and women entered my life
and became powers within me."

Who, apart from my parents,
became a power within me?

A candle
loses nothing by lighting another candle.

JAMES KELLER

WEDNESDAY
Ordinary Time
Week 10 _____

[Jesus said,]
"Whoever obeys the Law
and teaches others to do the same,
will be great
in the Kingdom of heaven."

MATTHEW 5:19

A high school girl tells this story.
One morning
her father was leaving for work.
He was about a half-hour early, as usual.
"Dad," she said, "why don't you relax
at home for an extra half-hour,
rather than go to work so early?"
Her father replied,
"I don't go to work immediately;
I usually catch the eight o'clock Mass
at Holy Trinity."
Later, the girl said to a friend,
"I was really impressed.
It gave me a new attitude toward Mass
and a new insight into my dad."

Do I really believe
that example speaks louder than words?
What does my example say to others,
especially about my faith?

Holy men and women serve this world
by reflecting in it the light of another.

JOHN W. DONOHUE

*[Jesus said,] "If you are about
to offer your gift to God at the altar
and there you remember that . . .
[someone] has something against you,
leave . . . make peace . . .
and then come back and offer your gift."*

MATTHEW 5:23-24

Mary Ehrlichmann's life
was plunged into an abyss of sorrow
when her husband was murdered
by three unknown hitchhikers.
After her grief reached its full depth,
she wrote an open letter
to the three slayers of her husband.
It read, in part:
"Please, if you see this,
find a church someplace
where you can be alone;
then read this again.
Know that God forgives you
and that my family and I forgive you—
then go out
and make something worthwhile
out of the rest of your lives."

What was one of the most difficult
acts of forgiveness for me to make?

Sins cannot be undone, only forgiven.

IGOR STRAVINSKY

FRIDAY
Ordinary Time
Week 10

[Jesus said,]
"You have heard that it was said,
'Do not commit adultery.'
But now I tell you:
anyone who looks at a woman
and wants to possess her
is guilty of committing adultery
with her in his heart."

MATTHEW 5:27-28

There's a delightful scene in *Peter Pan*.
Peter has just flown through the air.
The kids try to fly, too, but can't.
They ask Peter, "How do you do it?"
Peter says, "Think lovely thoughts.
They'll lift you up into the air."
Peter's advice surely
applies to today's gospel reading,
in which Jesus warns us
about sins of the mind.
One defense against mental sinfulness
is to follow Peter's advice:
"Think lovely thoughts.
They'll lift you into the air."

How do I handle mental temptations?

Good thoughts bear good fruit,
bad thoughts bear bad fruit—
and man is his own gardener.

JAMES ALLEN

[Jesus said,]
"Do not use any vow
when you make a promise. . . .
Just say 'Yes' or 'No.'"

MATTHEW 5:34, 37

A high school student
composed this "pencil" meditation:
"Every day,
as I hitchhike home from school,
I meet the same kind of drivers.
They motion that they are going to turn
so they won't have to pick you up.
Then as you watch,
they keep going in the same direction.
Lord, why don't people tell the truth?
Why don't they say 'no'
when they mean 'no'
and 'yes' when they mean 'yes'?"

On a scale of one (not very) to ten (very),
how truthful am I?

Cowardice asks . . . "Is it safe?"
Expedience asks . . . "Is it politic?"
Vanity asks . . . "Is it popular?" . . .
There comes a time
when one must take a position
that is neither safe, politic, nor popular,
but one must take it because it is right.

MARTIN LUTHER KING, JR.

SUNDAY
Ordinary Time
Week 11 _____

Jesus went around visiting
all the towns and villages. . . .
As he saw the crowds . . .
he said to his disciples,
"The harvest is large,
but there are few workers to gather it in."

MATTHEW 9:35-37

Imagine you are hired
by a team of advertising consultants.
Your job is to design
a television commercial
to run just before the half
at the Super Bowl.
Its purpose is to invite young people—
and older ones—
to consider a vocation to ministry
in the Church.

What would you do
to get the attention of TV viewers?
What would you say to them
once you got their attention?

Lord, in this critical moment
in human history,
bless the vineyard of your world
with men and women who will
teach in your Son's name,
walk in his footsteps, and
break bread in his memory.

[Jesus said,]
"You have heard that it was said,
'An eye for an eye,
and a tooth for a tooth.'
But now I tell you:
do not take revenge on someone
who wrongs you."

MATTHEW 5:38-39

A woman was shocked
when she heard Abraham Lincoln
speak kindly of the Confederate soldiers.
She challenged him, saying,
"I think we'd be better advised to focus
on destroying our enemies,
rather than befriending them."
Lincoln replied,
"Madam, we destroy our enemies
when we befriend them."
It is this kind
of wisdom and compassion
that permeates Jesus' teaching
in today's Scripture reading.

When was the last time
I prayed for an enemy
or reached out to an enemy?

The old law about "an eye for an eye"
leaves everybody blind.

MARTIN LUTHER KING, JR.

TUESDAY
Ordinary Time
Week 11 _____

[Jesus said,]
"You have heard that it was said,
'Love your friends, hate your enemies.'
But now I tell you: love your enemies."

MATTHEW 5:43–44

Years ago scientists held a seminar
involving creative experiments
for unlocking the potential in nature.
For example, one dealt with transmitting
200 TV programs simultaneously
on a cable the size of a human hair.
A person attending the seminar
noticed that no experiment dealt with
unlocking the potential in *human* nature.
Later, that person interviewed experts
on what they would recommend
to help people do this.
One expert's answer was unexpected:
"Love your enemies.
Do this and you'll discover
a potential for loving and forgiving
that you never dreamed you had."

What is one thing that keeps me
from loving and forgiving as Jesus taught?

If the scales of sin
ever fall from our eyes,
the world will begin to sparkle.

JOHN MICHAEL TALBOT (slightly adapted)

WEDNESDAY
Ordinary Time
Week 11

*[Jesus said,] "Do not perform
your religious duties in public
so that people will see what you do. . . .
So when you give something
to a needy person,
do not make a big show of it. . . .
And your Father,
who sees what you do in private,
will reward you."*

MATTHEW 6:1-2, 4

Dag Hammarskjold
was Secretary-General of the UN
from 1953 until 1961,
when he was killed in a plane crash.
His personal journal, *Markings*
(found in his apartment after his death),
contained this revealing entry:
"Uneasy, uneasy, uneasy—why? . . .
Because anxious for the good opinion
of others . . . you have lowered yourself
to wondering what will happen in the end
to what you have done."
Then he added, "Bless your uneasiness
as a sign that there is still life in you."

How much am I driven by a desire
to be recognized and honored by others?

*Lord, help me never to do the right thing
for the wrong reason.*

THURSDAY
Ordinary Time
Week 11 _____

[Jesus said to his disciples,]
"This, then, is how you should pray:
'Our Father in heaven:
May your holy name be honored;
may your Kingdom come.'"

MATTHEW 6:9-10

Dag Hammarskjold's personal journal
reveals him to be
a deeply prayerful person
even though he had no declared religion.
He was responsible for building
the Meditation Room at the UN.
One prayer that he meditated on a lot
is the Lord's Prayer.
His journal has several references to it,
including this one:
"Hallowed be Thy name, not mine,
Thy kingdom come, not mine,
Thy will be done, not mine."

What did Saint Augustine mean
when he wrote:
"What we ought to pray for
is in the Lord's Prayer;
what is not in it, we ought not pray for"?

The Lord's Prayer
may be committed to memory quickly,
but it is slowly learned by heart.

F. D. MAURICE

FRIDAY
Ordinary Time
Week 11

*[Jesus said,] "Do not store up riches
for yourselves here on earth. . . .
Instead, store up riches
for yourselves in heaven. . . .
For your heart will always be
where your riches are."*

MATTHEW 6:19-21

Natives seized a shipwrecked sailor,
took him to their village, set him
on a throne, and treated him as a king.
Then the sailor learned his fate.
He would be king for a year
and then taken to a barren island
to be left as an offering to the gods.
The sailor quickly devised a plan.
As king, he ordered
carpenters to build a boat,
farmers to plant gardens on the island,
and masons to construct buildings on it.
That story
makes a good parable of Christian life.
Like the shipwrecked sailor,
we know our future;
and we should be preparing for it wisely.

How wisely and carefully am I preparing
for my future?

Life is a voyage that's homeward bound.
HERMAN MELVILLE

SATURDAY
Ordinary Time
Week 11 _____

[Jesus said,]
"No one can be a slave of two masters."

MATTHEW 6:24

The play *A Man for All Seasons*
is the true story of Saint Thomas More.
In one scene, a friend pressures More
to sign a paper saying that the marriage
of Henry VIII to Anne Boleyn is lawful.
If More refuses to sign,
the king will execute him for treason.
Thomas More refuses,
for he thinks the marriage is unlawful.
His friend grows impatient, saying,
"Oh, confound all this. . . .
Frankly I don't know
whether the marriage is lawful or not.
But damn it, Thomas,
look at these names. . . .
You know these men! Can't you . . .
come along with us for fellowship?"
Thomas still refuses;
he won't serve two masters.

Where in my life
am I, perhaps, experiencing a pressure
to serve two masters?

"Son, never do a wrong thing
to make a friend or to keep one."

ROBERT E. LEE to his son at West Point

[Jesus said,]
"Do not be afraid of those who kill the body
but cannot kill the soul;
rather be afraid of God, who can destroy
both body and soul in hell."

MATTHEW 10:28

Dr. Sheila Cassidy went to Chile
to work among the poorest of the poor.
One day she treated an opposition leader.
The secret police learned about it,
arrested her, and tortured her.
She writes in *Audacity to Believe:*
"After four days of physical pain . . .
I was left completely alone
in a small room. . . .
Incredibly . . . I was filled with joy,
for I knew . . . that God was with me,
and that nothing they could do to me
could change that."
Sheila now understood Jesus' words,
"Do not be afraid of those who kill the body
but cannot kill the soul."

What am I most afraid of in my life?
What do I say to Jesus about it?

Lord, I do not ask
that I never be afflicted, but only
that you never abandon me in affliction.

SAINT BERNADETTE SOUBIROUS

MONDAY
Ordinary Time
Week 12 _____

*[Jesus said,] "Do not judge others,
so that God will not judge you,
for God will judge you
in the same way you judge others,
and [God] will apply to you
the same rules you apply to others."*

MATTHEW 7:1-2

An unknown poet writes:
"I dreamed death came the other night
And heaven's gate swung wide.
With kindly grace an angel
Ushered me inside.
And there to my astonishment
Stood folks I'd known on earth,
Some I'd judged and labeled
Unfit, of little worth.
Indignant words rose to my lips
But never were set free—
For every face showed stunned surprise;
Not one expected me."

How negative do I tend to be
in my judgment of people?
Anyone in particular? Why?

*Check your hand
the next time you point your finger
at somebody else.
Notice that three fingers
are pointing back at you.*

*[Jesus said,] "The gate to hell is wide
and the road that leads to it is easy. . . .
But the gate to life is narrow
and the way that leads to it is hard,
and there are few people who find it."*

MATTHEW 7:13-14

Sports Illustrated carried a story
about a Florida tennis school for teens.
It is run like a marine boot camp:
lights out at ten, no TV on weekdays.
Yet, teenagers flock through its
narrow gate to travel its hard road—
simply for the chance to excel in tennis.
Their commitment recalls Paul's words:
"Every athlete in training
submits to strict discipline,
in order to be crowned with a wreath
that will not last;
but we do it for one
that will last forever."

1 CORINTHIANS 9:25

To what degree am I more committed
to working for
a material wreath that will not last,
than for a spiritual one that will?

*If sunbeams were weapons of war,
we would have had solar energy centuries ago.*

NOBEL LAUREATE SIR GEORGE POTTS

WEDNESDAY
Ordinary Time
Week 12 _____

*[Jesus warned,] "Be on your guard
against false prophets. . . .
You will know them by what they do."*
MATTHEW 7:15-16

Two Cleveland teenagers
got an idea for a unique comic strip.
They tried to sell it
to a number of editors.
All rejected it for the same reason:
the main character was too foolish.
The teenagers
finally gave up on the idea
and sold their rights to it for $130.
That comic strip idea was Superman.
The so-called experts
turned out to be false prophets.
Because the teenagers believed them,
they sold a treasure for a pittance.

There are experts today who say it is foolish
to live by Jesus' teachings.
They say it is foolish
to put your faith in a person
who lived 2,000 years ago.
To what extent—and how—
might I be influenced by them?

*Live today the way you will wish
you had lived
when you stand in judgment before God.*

[Jesus said to his disciples,]
"Who hears these words of mine
and does not obey them
is like a foolish man
who built his house on sand.
The rain poured down,
the rivers flooded over,
the wind blew hard against that house,
and it fell.
And what a terrible fall that was!"

MATTHEW 7:26-27

Hubert Courtney
was on trial for interstate auto theft.
In an effort to help his case,
he removed his shirt
and showed everyone his chest.
It contained a colorful tattoo reading
"Crime does not pay."
No one was impressed.

The story of Courtney
and the words of Jesus invite me to ask:
What is one action in my own life
that is somewhat inconsistent
with what I profess to believe?
What might I do about it?

Knowing the truth and not doing it
is as foolish as writing a love letter
and not mailing it.

FRIDAY
Ordinary Time
Week 12 _____

[A leper said to Jesus,]
"If you want to, you can make me clean."
Jesus reached out and touched him.
"I do want to," he answered. "Be clean!"
At once the man was healed.

MATTHEW 8:2-3

A chemistry teacher told a friend
how he spends his vacations.
He flies to India at his own expense,
goes into rural areas, and teaches lepers
to make ointments from local vegetation
to ease their disease.
The friend was deeply moved.
She said later, "It spoke to me
of Jesus' own love for lepers."

An aboriginal Australian woman said:
"If you have come to help me,
you are wasting your time.
But if you have come
because your liberation is bound up
with mine, then let us work together."
The woman's remark invites me
to ask myself: What did she mean,
and how does it apply to me?

Our lives no longer belong to us alone;
they belong to all
who need us desperately.

ELIE WIESEL

*[When Jesus offered to go to the home
of a Roman officer to heal his servant,
the officer said,] "Just give the order,
and my servant will get well. . . ."
When Jesus heard this, he was surprised
and said to the people following him,
"I tell you, I have never found
anyone in Israel with faith like this."*

MATTHEW 8:8, 10

A rural schoolteacher
reminded her children daily
of Jesus' readiness to help us
in critical situations.
One winter day a blizzard struck.
The teacher dismissed class early
and began to lead the children
through the blowing snow and wind.
Before long, she was, literally,
pulling them through the deep snow.
Suddenly, one little boy said to her,
"I think it's time to call on Jesus."

Can I recall any time
when, after doing all that I could,
I turned to Jesus for extra help?
With what results?

*Prayer is an expression of who we are. . . .
We are living incompleteness.*

THOMAS MERTON

SUNDAY
Ordinary Time
Week 13 _____

[Jesus said,]
"Whoever does not take up his cross
and follow in my steps
is not fit to be my disciple."

MATTHEW 10:38

A scene in the film *American Anthem*
shows a young man who can't accept
the fact that he lost a leg in an accident.
He draws the blinds of his room,
lets nobody in, and passes his time
in darkness, listening to music.
Contrast this scene with another scene
reported by Robert Bruce.
Walking along a crowded street,
Bruce heard someone singing joyfully.
When he located the source,
he couldn't believe his eyes.
It was a legless man,
pushing himself along in a wheelchair.
One person's rejection of a cross
brought sadness;
the other's acceptance of it brought joy.

What is one cross in my life
that I am finding hard to accept?

I thank God for my handicaps,
for through them, I have found
myself, my work, and my God.
HELEN KELLER

MONDAY
Ordinary Time
Week 13

[A young person delayed accepting
Jesus' invitation to be a disciple, saying,
"First let me . . . bury my father."
[Jesus responded by saying,]
"Let the dead bury their own dead."

MATTHEW 8:21-22

To the Western mind,
Jesus' words sound almost cruel,
but they fit the Eastern context.
For example, a young Arab once refused
a college scholarship, saying,
"I'll take it only after I bury my father."
His father was healthy and under fifty.
The boy wanted to put off leaving home
until his father's death.
His father might need him in old age.

Jesus' point is this:
Even the noblest reason is no excuse
for putting off following him.
It invites me to ask myself:
To what extent am I putting off
following Jesus more closely?

There is a tide in the affairs of men,
Which, taken at the flood,
leads on to fortune;
Omitted, all the voyage of their life
Is bound in shallows and in miseries.

WILLIAM SHAKESPEARE, *Julius Caesar*

TUESDAY
Ordinary Time
Week 13 _____

*[Jesus and his disciples were out at sea,
when suddenly a storm blew up,
threatening to sink their boat. Jesus]
got up and ordered the winds and the waves
to stop, and there was a great calm.*

MATTHEW 8:26

John Newton was a slave trader.
One night a storm blew up,
threatening to sink his slave ship.
John cried out to God,
"Save us, and I'll quit this business
and become your slave forever."
The ship survived. John quit the trade
and became a minister of the Gospel.
To celebrate his conversion,
he wrote these words of a famous song:
"Amazing grace; how sweet the sound
That saved a wretch like me!
I once was lost, but now am found—
Was blind, but now I see."

When did Jesus help me
through a "stormy" situation in my life?
Generally, do "storms" lead me closer to
or further away from Christ? Why?

*[The disciples cried out in amazement,]
"What kind of man is this? . . .
Even the winds and the waves obey him!"*

MATTHEW 8:27

[Jesus expelled demons from two men.
The demons entered some pigs,
causing them to leap into the sea.
Disturbed by these events, the people]
begged [Jesus] to leave their territory.

MATTHEW 8:34

A last-minute concert assignment
forced a music critic to cancel
a dinner date with some friends.
Then the soloist's son died suddenly,
causing the concert to be postponed.
The critic phoned his friends, saying,
"Good news! The soloist's son died,
so the concert is postponed."
Suddenly he realized what he had said.
The son's death was not "good news";
it was "tragic news."
Something similar happens in the Gospel.
Jesus restores two men to sanity,
at the cost of a few pigs.
But the people are more concerned
about the pigs than the men.
So they ask Jesus to go away.

Do I ever let routine concerns blind me
to the life-death concerns of others?

When you betray somebody else,
you also betray yourself.

ISAAC SINGER

THURSDAY
Ordinary Time
Week 13 _____

[Some people brought Jesus a paralytic.
When Jesus saw their faith,
he said to the paralytic,]
"Your sins are forgiven. . . .
Get up, pick up your bed, and go home!"

MATTHEW 9:2, 6

A high school girl imagined herself
to be the paralytic brought to Jesus.
She describes her feelings:
"Suddenly I began to feel bad
about what I had done in my life.
I had the feeling
this person knew all about me.
His voice matched his eyes.
It was a voice that could calm a child,
yet shake a building.
He told me my sins were forgiven.
How could I not believe that voice—
and those eyes?
I *knew* my sins were forgiven."
(slightly adapted)

How deeply do I believe
that Jesus wants to forgive all my sins?
How ready am I to forgive others,
as Jesus has forgiven me?

Who forgives most
will be most forgiven.
WILLIAM W. BAILEY

*[Some Pharisees were complaining
because Jesus ate with outcasts.]
Jesus heard them and answered,
"People who are well do not need
a doctor, but only those who are sick."*
MATTHEW 9:12

A window washer who washed
only clean windows would be a fool.
A relief agency that helped
only wealthy people would be a laugh.
A hospital that treated
only healthy patients would be a joke.
This is Jesus' point in today's reading.
Why should people be amazed
to find him ministering
to outcasts and sinners?
The fact that the Pharisees were amazed
shows how far they had drifted from
exercising true religious leadership.

Who are some sinners and outcasts today
that Jesus would minister to?
To what extent, and how,
might I let Jesus do this through me?

*It is the greatest of all mistakes
to do nothing
because you can only do a little.
Do what you can.*
SYDNEY SMITH

SATURDAY
Ordinary Time
Week 13 _____

*[Someone asked Jesus why his disciples
didn't fast. Jesus responded,]*
*"Do you expect the guests
at a wedding party to be sad
as long as the bridegroom is with them?
Of course not!"*
MATTHEW 9:15

A woman cut a slice of meat
from the ends of a ham before baking it.
Her husband asked, "Why'd you do that?"
"I really don't know," she said,
"but my mother always did it."
The next time she saw her mother,
she asked her about the practice.
Her mother said, "I did it because
the butcher's hams were always
about an inch longer than my baking pan."

In Jesus' day, people fasted
to prepare for the Messiah's coming.
Now the Messiah had come.
To continue to fast was as meaningless
as cutting off the ends of a ham
when a larger pan is available.
To what extent
do I hold on to practices uncritically?

*Practice without thought is blind;
thought without practice is empty.*
KWAME NKRUMAH

SUNDAY
Ordinary Time
Week 14

[Jesus said,] "Learn from me,
because I am gentle and humble in spirit;
and you will find rest.
For the yoke I will give you is easy,
and the load I will put on you is light."

MATTHEW 11:29-30

Roger Bolduc died in Waterville, Maine,
after a long bout with cancer.
He saw his illness as a gift from God.
Shortly before dying, he wrote:
"Many things upon which
I placed importance in the past
seem so trivial now. . . .
God has become so real. . . .
I have always felt close to God,
but I feel even closer now. I feel
that he loves me more than ever. . . .
I can feel his power—it's always there.
I feel that God has answered
my prayers. . . . I feel loved."

What are some "loads" or "crosses"
I have had to carry in my lifetime?
Did any of these turn into a blessing?

You may not realize it when it happens,
but a kick in the teeth
may be the best thing in the world
for you.

WALT DISNEY

MONDAY
Ordinary Time
Week 14

[Believing she would be healed,
a sick woman touched Jesus' cloak.]
Jesus turned around and saw her,
and said, "Courage my daughter!"
At that very moment
the woman became well.

MATTHEW 9:22

Before she was converted
and began working among the poor,
Dorothy Day spent many a night
in New York's bars. On her way home,
she would often stop in at early Mass
at St. Joseph's on Sixth Avenue.
What drew her were the people there
kneeling in prayer. She writes
in *From Union Square to Rome*:
"I seemed to feel
the faith of those about me
and I longed for their faith. . . .
So I used to go in . . .
and perhaps I asked even then,
'God be merciful to me a sinner.' "

The "faith stories" of the sick woman
and of Dorothy Day invite me to reflect
on my own faith story.
What were some of its milestones?

"I believe; help my unbelief!"
MARK 9:24 (NRSV)

TUESDAY
Ordinary Time
Week 14

*[Seeing the crowds of people
in search of truth and guidance,
Jesus] said to his disciples,
"The harvest is large,
but there are few workers
to gather it in."* MATTHEW 9:37

A photo in the Sunday newspaper
showed a field of strawberries rotting.
The caption read:
"Tons of strawberries will rot because
few workers can be found to pick them."
The scene of the rotting berries
brings to mind a more tragic scene:
millions of people in our world
waiting for someone to bring them
the truth and guidance of the Gospel.
If Jesus were to write a caption
for this tragic scene, it might read:
"I have no feet but your feet
to take me into your world.
I have no tongue but your tongue
to tell people why I died for them."

What is one response
that I might make
to the caption that Jesus might write?

Think globally, but act locally.

Motto posted in Coca-Cola Headquarters

WEDNESDAY
Ordinary Time
Week 14

[Jesus sent forth twelve disciples,
saying to them,] "Go and preach,
'The Kingdom of heaven is near!' "

MATTHEW 10:7

An artist was painting a picture
illustrating these lines of a hymn:
"Around the throne of God in heaven
Thousands of children stand."
After days of work, she completed it.
Exhausted, she fell asleep.
During the night she heard a noise.
A stranger was repainting her picture.
"Stop!" she shouted. "You're ruining it."
"It's ruined already," said the stranger.
"I'm trying to save it by painting
the children's faces different colors."
Then the artist awoke.
She realized that it was Jesus
who had spoken to her in a dream.
God's Kingdom began in Palestine,
like a tiny mustard seed;
but he intends his followers to spread it
to every nation and every race.

What is one way I spread God's Kingdom?

I am a little pencil
in the hands of a writing God
who is sending a love letter to the world.

MOTHER TERESA

THURSDAY
Ordinary Time
Week 14

[Jesus said,]
"You have received without paying,
so give without being paid."

MATTHEW 10:8

Geraldine Marshall
says that her favorite birthday memory
is not one of her own, but of her dad's.
One day in her childhood,
her dad gave her a stuffed tiger.
She jumped up and down for joy.
Then, suddenly, she stopped and said,
"But, Daddy, it's your birthday, not mine.
Why did you give me a gift?
I should give you a gift."
Her father replied,
"You have given me a marvelous gift:
your happiness with my gift."
Geraldine still has that stuffed tiger.
But the most precious gift
her father gave her that day
was an insight into the joy of giving.

What is a recent gift from someone
that meant a lot to me? Why?
What is a recent gift I gave someone
that meant a lot to him or her?

The fragrance always stays
in the hand that gives the rose.

HADA BEJAR

FRIDAY
Ordinary Time
Week 14 _____

*[Jesus said,] "I am sending you out
just like sheep to a pack of wolves. . . .
But whoever holds out to the end
will be saved."*

MATTHEW 10:16, 22

An old Roman coin bears an image
of an ox gazing at an altar and a plow.
Beneath the image is this inscription:
"Ready for either."
The Roman ox was not only a beast
of burden but also a beast of sacrifice.
It had to be ready for
either a short life ending in bloodshed
or a long, hard life of pulling a plow.
The first Roman Christians
were a lot like the Roman ox.
They too had to be ready for a short life,
ending in bloodshed (martyrdom), or
a long, hard life of
pulling the plow (witnessing to Jesus).

The fate of the first Roman Christians
could easily become
that of modern Christians as well.
How prepared am I for such a fate?

*The only ultimate disaster
that can befall us . . . is to feel ourselves
to be at home here on earth.*

MALCOLM MUGGERIDGE

[Jesus told his disciples,]
"Do not be afraid of those who kill
the body but cannot kill the soul;
rather be afraid of God, who can destroy
both body and soul in hell."

MATTHEW 10:28

One Sunday, the king of England
showed up unannounced at the church
of a famous English pastor.
When the pastor saw the king,
he grew alarmed.
For his planned remarks were quite blunt
about the rich and the powerful
who ignored the poor—
something the king was guilty of.
So before he started to preach,
he paused and spoke out loud to himself:
"O, pastor, be careful what you say.
The king of England is here today."
Then pausing again, he said, "Oh, pastor,
be careful what you *don't* say.
The King of Kings is also here today."

Jesus spoke out fearlessly against evil.
No one intimidated him.
How fearlessly do I speak out against evil?

Courage is doing what you're afraid to do.
There is no courage unless you're scared.

EDDIE RICKENBACKER

SUNDAY
Ordinary Time
Week 15 _____

[Jesus said to his disciples,]
"How fortunate you are! . . .
Many of God's people
wanted very much to see what you see,
but they could not, and
to hear what you hear, but they did not."

MATTHEW 13:16-17

After fire destroyed his mansion,
basketball star Kareem Abdul-Jabbar
told reporters:
"My whole perspective changed. . . .
I think it's important now for me
to spend time with my son Amir
and appreciate other things
besides basketball."
Kareem was fortunate. He heard
what many people have never heard:
God's voice speaking to him
through events.
He saw what many have never seen:
that life contains more important things
than fame or money.

Can I recall a time when God seemed
to speak to me?
What did God seem to say?

God often visits us,
but most of the time we are not at home.

JOSEPH ROUX

[Jesus said,] "Whoever loves . . .
father or mother more than me
is not fit to be my disciple."

MATTHEW 10:37

A great biblical friendship
was between David and Jonathan,
the son of King Saul.
One day King Saul ordered his son
to betray David, but Jonathan refused.
Jonathan's refusal
illustrates Jesus' point in today's gospel:
When it comes to right or wrong,
not even our parents
can force us to violate our conscience.
Our decision to follow Jesus falls
into this category of right and wrong.
No one can interfere with it,
not even our father or our mother.

Jesus' point invites me to ask myself:
To what extent do my friends—
even my family—interfere with
my following of Jesus? Help it?

It's the age-old struggle—
the roar of the crowd
on one side
and the voice of your conscience
on the other.

GENERAL DOUGLAS MACARTHUR

TUESDAY
Ordinary Time
Week 15 _____

The people in the towns
where Jesus had performed
most of his miracles
did not turn from their sins,
so he reproached those towns.
"How terrible
it will be for you, Chorazin!
How terrible for you too, Bethsaida! . . .
On the Judgment Day God will show
more mercy to Sodom than to you!"

MATTHEW 11:20-21, 24

A few miles from the Sea of Galilee
are the ruins of ancient Chorazin.
As you sit silently amidst the ruins,
you can almost hear the voice of Jesus
echoing across the centuries:
"How terrible . . . for you, Chorazin!"
The echoing voice of Jesus
invites me to ask:
How will it be for me
when my life ends?

After we have brushed off
the dust and chips of life,
we will have left
only the hard, clean question:
Was it good or was it evil?
Have we done well—or ill?

JOHN STEINBECK (slightly adapted)

Jesus said, "Father, . . .
you have shown to the unlearned
what you have hidden from the wise."

MATTHEW 11:25

A test for astronaut candidates
included giving 20 answers
to this question: "Who are you?"
John Glenn says, "The first few answers
were easy: 'I'm a man!' 'I'm a pilot!'
'I'm an American!' Then it got harder."
Glenn's observation
touches on an important point:
We can know a lot *about ourselves,*
but not *know ourselves.*
It's the same with knowing God.
We can know a lot *about God,*
but not *know God.*
Jesus had this in mind when he praised
his Father for revealing to the unlearned
what he had hidden from the learned.

Knowing about God is an activity of the head.
Knowing God is an activity of the heart.
This raises a question:
How does *head* knowledge
differ from *heart* knowledge?

Knowing God is not so much a question
of opening a book and reading about God,
but of opening the heart and loving God.

THURSDAY
Ordinary Time
Week 15 _____

[Jesus said,]
"Take my yoke and put it on you. . . .
For the yoke I will give you is easy,
and the load I will put on you is light."

MATTHEW 11:29-30

A yoke is a wooden harness
used to join the necks of two oxen
so that they can pull a load together.
Carpenters shaped the yoke to fit
each animal to avoid painful rubbing.
Legend says Jesus made yokes
in the carpenter shop at Nazareth.
So he knew what he was talking about
when he said, "My yoke is easy."
The word Jesus used for "easy"
may also be translated "well fitting."
In other words, Jesus is saying,
"Trust me, and yoke yourself to me.
Together we can pull any load."

What is one thing
that keeps me from trusting
that Jesus and I can pull any load?

We shall steer safely
through every storm,
so long as our heart is right,
our intention is fervent . . .
and our trust is fixed firmly on God.

SAINT FRANCIS DE SALES

FRIDAY
Ordinary Time
Week 15

[Jesus said to some Pharisees,
who were worried more about the letter
of the law than its spirit,]
"The scripture says, 'It is kindness
that I want, not animal sacrifices.' "

MATTHEW 12:7

Imagine you gave a birthday party
for your little daughter.
Imagine that as she unwrapped each gift
she kept the paper and trashed the gift.
This absurd example gives us an insight
into what some Pharisees were doing.
They were turning religion into something
God never intended it to be.
They were keeping the paper (God's laws)
and trashing the gift (God's love).

The words of Jesus in today's reading
invite me to ask myself:
To what extent
might I be in danger of doing
what the Pharisees were doing:
trashing the gift of God's love and
keeping the paper it was wrapped in?

Lord, help me to realize
that religion is not a list of things to do,
but a person to be followed.
It is not a set of laws to be followed,
but a life of love to be lived.

SATURDAY
Ordinary Time
Week 15 _____

[Isaiah said of the Messiah,]
"He will be gentle to those who are weak,
and kind to those who are helpless."

MATTHEW 12:20

The sun and the wind were arguing
about who was stronger, when a chance
to settle their argument arose.
A person wearing a coat
was walking down a country road.
They agreed that whoever
could make the person remove the coat faster
would be declared the winner.
The wind went first; it blew and blew.
But the more it blew,
the tighter the person buttoned the coat.
The sun went next.
It merely shone in all its glory.
Shortly, the person removed the coat.

The point of that ancient fable is this:
More can be achieved by gentleness
than by violence.
The fable's point invites me to ask:
What is one way
that I might become gentler in my life?

What comes from the heart
touches the heart.

DON SIBET

*[Jesus said, "An enemy sowed weeds
in a farmer's field. When the farmer saw the
weeds growing amid the wheat,
he told his workers, 'Let the two plants]
grow together until harvest.
Then I will tell the harvest workers
to pull up the weeds . . . and burn them,
and then to gather in the wheat
and put it in my barn.'"*
MATTHEW 13:30

The wheat stands for good people;
the weeds stand for evil people.
Jesus' parable reminds me
that I should not be disturbed
to find "weeds" growing amid the "wheat"
in Jesus' Church.

What is/should be my attitude
toward the "weeds" growing
amid the wheat in Jesus' Church?

*Be patient with the Church.
It is always a community
of weak and imperfect individuals. . . .
Put yourself
at the disposal of the Church. . . .
The Church needs you. . . .
You are the future of the Church.*

POPE JOHN PAUL II,
speaking to the youth of Switzerland

MONDAY
Ordinary Time
Week 16

*[When people asked Jesus
for a special sign to authenticate
his claims, he refused,
saying that no sign would be given
except the sign of the prophet Jonah.
Jesus then added,] "In the same way
that Jonah spent three days and nights
in the big fish, so will the Son of Man
spend three days and nights
in the depths of the earth."*

MATTHEW 12:40

Gideon was a nobody
when God called him to lead Israel.
To make sure God was *really* calling him,
Gideon asked for a sign.
He put some wool outside and asked God
to cover it with dew in the morning,
while keeping the ground around it dry.
When God obliged, Gideon still doubted.
Gideon's story makes an important point:
signs cannot take the place of faith.

Why do I find it hard to have faith
at times?

*Come to the edge. No, we will fall!
Come to the edge. No, we will fall!
They came to the edge.
He pushed them, and they flew.*

SAINT APOLLINARIS

TUESDAY
Ordinary Time
Week 16

*[Jesus said,] "Whoever does
what my Father in heaven wants . . .
is my brother, my sister, and my mother."*
MATTHEW 12:50

A crisis led a person to pray
for the first time in years.
The person said:
"I committed myself to God . . .
[believing that God] would take all
from me, and I was willing. . . .
Since I gave up to God
all ownership of my life,
God has guided me . . .
in a way almost incredible
to those who do not enjoy the secret
of a truly surrendered life."
It is this kind of commitment
that Jesus talks about in today's gospel.

Jesus' words and the person's commitment
invite me to ask:
How willing am I to let God use me
for whatever purpose God might wish?
What are some fears I have about this?

*We have nothing of our own but our will.
It is the one thing
that God has so placed in our own power
that we can make an offering of it.*
SAINT JOHN VIANNEY

WEDNESDAY
Ordinary Time
Week 16 _____

The crowd that gathered around [Jesus]
was so large that he got into a boat
and sat in it, while the crowd
stood on the shore. [Jesus] used parables
to tell them many things.

MATTHEW 13:2-3

Parables were ideal for teaching people
about such things as God's Kingdom
and the Messiah. How so?
Many people expected God's Kingdom
to be a worldly one that would make Israel
"number one" among the nations.
So too, they expected the Messiah
to be a worldly one
who would wear a crown of gold,
not a crown of thorns.
Jesus had to correct these false ideas.
This required tact.
That's why parables were ideal.
They redirected people's thinking
delicately, gradually, and sensitively.

What is one way I could be more delicate
and sensitive toward people around me,
especially those closest to me?

The wise person
doesn't give the right answers,
but poses the right questions.
  CLAUDE LEVI-STRAUSS (slightly adapted)

[Jesus said,]
"The prophecy of Isaiah applies to them:
'This people will listen and listen,
but not understand;
they will look and look, but not see,
because . . . they have stopped up
their ears and have closed their eyes.' "

MATTHEW 13:14-15

Author Arthur Gordon tells how his
Scout leader used to take them on hikes.
After walking ten minutes,
they would stop and the leader would say,
"Tell me what you saw and heard."
Invariably, it was only a fraction
of what he had seen and heard.
And he'd say, "Creation is everywhere,
but you're shutting it out. . . .
Stop wearing a raincoat in the shower!"
This ludicrous image applied to people
in Jesus' time also.
They heard but didn't listen.
They looked but didn't see.

To what extent might I be guilty
of "wearing a raincoat in the shower"?
Concerning what things? Persons?

Only the person who sees the invisible
can do the impossible.

FRANK GAINES (slightly adapted)

FRIDAY
Ordinary Time
Week 16 _____

[Jesus said,]
"Listen, then, and learn
what the parable of the sower means. . . .
The seeds that fell among thorn bushes
stand for those who hear the message;
but the worries about this life
and the love for riches
choke the message,
and they don't bear fruit."

MATTHEW 13:18, 22

A high school girl wrote:
"At the end of last year
I had a great talk with my counselor.
She helped me
see a lot of things differently.
As a result,
I made several resolutions.
Then, yesterday, it hit me.
I hadn't followed up
on a single resolution.
I had let all of them get lost
in a lot of other things."

The girl's experience invites me to ask:
What is one way that I tend to be
like the seed that fell among the thorns?

I think God's going to come down
and pull civilization over for speeding.
STEVEN WRIGHT

*[Jesus said, "An enemy
sowed weeds in a farmer's field.
The farmer told his workers,]
'Let the wheat and the weeds
both grow together until harvest.
Then I will tell the harvest workers
to pull up the weeds . . . and burn them.'"*

MATTHEW 13:30

Pointing to a gang of street toughs,
Susan said to her Christian friend, Kay,
"It's been 2,000 years
since your Jesus came into the world,
and it's still filled with evil people.
He didn't change anything."
Five minutes later,
the two friends came upon a group
of dirty-faced children.
Kay turned to Susan and said,
"It's been 2,000 years
since soap was discovered in our world,
and it's still filled with dirty faces."

How does the story of Susan and Kay
help to give me a better insight
into why there is still so much evil
in our world?

*Do what you can,
with what you have, where you are.*

THEODORE ROOSEVELT

SUNDAY
Ordinary Time
Week 17 _____

[Jesus said,]
"The Kingdom of heaven is like this.
A man happens to find a treasure
hidden in a field. . . .
He goes and sells everything he has,
and then goes back and buys that field."

MATTHEW 13:44

An elderly lady in Scotland was so poor
her neighbors had to support her.
They were happy to do this,
but what bothered some of them
was that her son had gone to America
and become rich.
The mother defended her son, saying,
"He writes me every week
and always sends me a little picture.
See," she said,
"I keep them in my Bible."
Between the pages of her Bible
were hundreds of U.S. bank notes.
The woman had a treasure in her Bible,
but didn't realize it.

To what extent
do I need to rediscover the treasure
in my Bible: Jesus Christ?

Christ is not valued at all
unless he is valued above all.
SAINT AUGUSTINE

Jesus told them another parable:
"The Kingdom of heaven is like this.
A man takes a mustard seed
and sows it in his field.
It is the smallest of all seeds,
but when it grows up, it is the biggest
of all plants. It becomes a tree,
so that birds come
and make their nests in its branches."

MATTHEW 13:31-32

A mother gave her son an acorn, saying,
"The tree we are sitting under
was once a tiny acorn like this."
The little boy looked at the tree;
then he looked at the acorn again.
"Mommy," he said, "how can God pack
such a big tree into such a tiny acorn?"
Jesus' disciples also wondered
how the tiny group of Jesus' followers
could grow into a worldwide Church.

To what extent
do I tend to view things and people
from a purely human viewpoint,
forgetting about the divine viewpoint?
What one thing or person, especially?

Lord, help me look at acorns and see trees.
Help me look at raindrops and see oceans.
Help me look at time and see eternity.

TUESDAY
Ordinary Time
Week 17 _____

[One day Jesus' disciples said,]
"Tell us what the parable
about the weeds in the field means."
Jesus answered,
"The man who sowed the good seed
is the Son of Man; the field is the world;
the good seed is the people
who belong to the Kingdom;
the weeds are the people who belong
to the Evil One; and the enemy
who sowed the weeds is the Devil."

MATTHEW 13:36-39

A Greek philosopher was carrying
a lighted lantern in broad daylight.
When asked about this, the philosopher said,
"I'm looking for an honest person."
Perhaps I may feel like the philosopher.
I see so much graft in our world that
I wonder if any honest people are left.
Jesus warned this would be the case.
He foretold
that the wheat field of God's Kingdom
would also be riddled with weeds.

What is one way that weeds in God's Kingdom
tend to impact my faith?

Do not let evil defeat you;
instead, conquer evil with good.

ROMANS 12:21

WEDNESDAY
Ordinary Time
Week 17

[Jesus said,]
"The Kingdom of heaven is like this.
A man is looking for fine pearls, and
when he finds one that is unusually fine,
he goes and sells everything he has,
and buys that pearl."

MATTHEW 13:45-46

Someone asked Ignace Paderewski,
the famed concert pianist,
why he continued to practice daily.
He answered,
"If I skip one day, I notice it.
If I skip two days, critics notice it.
If I skip three days, audiences notice it."
The same is true
about my following of Jesus.
I've found the great pearl, who is Jesus.
Following Jesus invites total dedication.
If I hold back one day, I notice it.
If I hold back two days, friends notice it.
If I hold back three days, all notice it.

What is one thing, especially,
that makes me want to follow Jesus
more closely than I have been doing
in the past?

Alas for those who never sing,
but die with their music within them.
OLIVER WENDELL HOLMES

THURSDAY
Ordinary Time
Week 17 _____

"The Kingdom of heaven is like this.
Some fishermen
throw their net out in the lake
and catch all kinds of fish.
When the net is full, they pull it to shore
and sit down to divide the fish:
the good ones go into the buckets,
the worthless ones are thrown away.
It will be like this at the end of the age."

MATTHEW 13:47-49

The Church is like a net
that fishermen cast into the sea.
The Church can't discriminate either.
Like a net,
it is open to everyone in its path:
good people and bad people,
selfless people and selfish people,
thoughtful people and thoughtless people.
Therefore, when we find people like this
in the Church, we should not be disturbed.
Jesus said that it would be this way.

How should I react to church people
who seem to live one life in church
and another life outside of church?

If you find a perfect church,
by all means join it!
Then it will no longer be perfect.

BILLY GRAHAM

FRIDAY
Ordinary Time
Week 17

[Jesus] taught in the synagogue, and
those who heard him were amazed. . . .
"Isn't he the carpenter's son?
Isn't Mary his mother . . . ?
Where did he get all this?"
And so they rejected him.

MATTHEW 13:54-57

Imagine someone asked you,
"When it comes to the communication
of God's Word in the Church,
who's the key person involved:
the preacher or you?
You would probably answer,
"Both of us are key!"—and you'd be right.
Your *openness* to the preacher's words
is as important as the words are.
If your heart is closed to the words,
you'll hear them one way.
If you're open to them,
you'll hear them another way.
More importantly, if you're open to them,
the Holy Spirit will be able to use them
to touch your heart—even if
the preacher's words lack eloquence.

What was one homily
that touched me rather deeply? Why?

"Speak, LORD, your servant is listening."

1 SAMUEL 3:9

SATURDAY
Ordinary Time
Week 17 _____

On Herod's birthday
the daughter of Herodias danced
in front of the whole group.
Herod was so pleased that he promised her,
"I . . . will give you anything you ask for!"
At her mother's suggestion
she asked him, "Give me . . . the head
of John the Baptist on a plate!" . . .
The head was brought in on a plate
and given to the girl.

MATTHEW 14:6-8, 11

This gospel event is incredible,
but similar events still happen.
For example, a 41-year-old father
drove to a California restaurant,
walked in, and gunned down 40 people.
We can't make sense of such insanity.
The best we can do is recall that Jesus
entered our world because of this insanity.
He began the battle against it,
but he left to us, his Church,
the task of completing his work.

What convinces me
that we will someday win the battle
over evil and all its insanity?

[Jesus promised his disciples,] "I will be
with you always, to the end of the age."

MATTHEW 28:20

*[A crowd
had been listening to Jesus all day.]
His disciples came to him and said,
"It is already very late. . . .
Send the people away . . .
to buy food for themselves.". . .
[Jesus replied,] "You yourselves
give them something to eat!"*

MATTHEW 14:15-16

A Christmas edition of *Newsweek*
ran this advertisement for victims
of a famine in Ethiopia: "Right now
giant cargo planes are delivering
enough food to feed tens of thousands
of hungry people a day. . . .
Here's how you can help!
Your gift of $15 is all it takes
to feed a hungry child for a month! . . .
Please give whatever you can—now!"

What is one thing that tends to keep me
from helping victims like this?

*["People will say at the Last Judgment,]
'When, Lord, did we ever see you hungry
and feed you?' . . . The King will reply,
'I tell you, whenever you did this for
one of the least important of these . . .
you did it for me!'"*

MATTHEW 25:37, 40

MONDAY
Ordinary Time
Week 18 _____

[During a storm at sea, Jesus appeared,
walking the waves toward his disciples.
Thinking it could be a ghost, Peter said,]
"Lord, if it is really you,
order me to come out on the water to you."
"Come!" answered Jesus.
So Peter got out of the boat. . . .
But when he noticed the strong wind,
he was afraid and started to sink. . . .
Jesus . . . grabbed hold of him and said,
"What little faith you have!
Why did you doubt?" MATTHEW 14:28-31

In the early days of sailing,
a boy was on his first training voyage.
He was assigned to climb the mast.
Halfway up he made the mistake
of looking down and became dizzy.
He was in serious danger of falling.
An old sailor called out to him,
"Look up, lad! Look up, lad!"
The boy obeyed and resumed the climb.
Peter made the same mistake as the boy.
He focused on the storm, not on the goal.

When things get stormy in life,
do I focus on the storm or on Jesus?

Have faith. . . . Trust in the LORD.
PSALM 27:14

TUESDAY
Ordinary Time
Week 18

Jesus called the crowd to him
and said to them,
"Listen and understand!
It is not what goes into a person's mouth
that makes him ritually unclean;
rather, what comes out of it. . . ."
Then the disciples came to him
and said,
"Do you know that the Pharisees
had their feelings hurt by what you said?"

MATTHEW 15:10-12

The Pharisees fell into the error
of identifying religion and pleasing God
with observing dietary laws,
such as abstaining from certain foods.
Jesus had to correct this error,
no matter whose feelings it hurt.
Religion has to do with the state
of a person's heart, not with diet.

If Jesus asked me about the state
of my heart, what would I say to him?

It is very much easier
to abstain from certain foods . . .
than it is to love the unlovely . . .
and to help the needy
at the cost of one's own . . .
comfort and pleasure.

WILLIAM BARCLAY

WEDNESDAY
Ordinary Time
Week 18 _____

[A pagan woman approached Jesus.
She began making a nuisance of herself,
trying to get Jesus to heal her daughter.
The disciples tried to get her to leave.
Even Jesus was slow to deal with her.
But she kept pressing her case.
Finally, Jesus said,]
"You are a woman of great faith!
What you want will be done for you."
And at that very moment
her daughter was healed.

MATTHEW 15:28

Parry O'Brien was an Olympic champion.
One night Parry's father was awakened
at 3:00 A.M. by a series of thuds.
Going to the window, he saw Parry
under the streetlight, heaving the shot.
"What are you doing?" he shouted.
Parry replied, "I got an idea
on how to throw the shot better.
I couldn't wait till morning to try it out."
Parry and the woman in the Gospel
had something in common: a determination
that was not easily discouraged.

How easily do I become discouraged?

By perseverance.
the snail reached the ark.
CHARLES SPURGEON

THURSDAY
Ordinary Time
Week 18

[One day Jesus asked his disciples,]
"Who do you say I am?"
Simon Peter answered, "You are
the Messiah, the Son of the living God."
"Good for you, Simon, son of John! . . .
For this truth did not come to you
from any human being,
but it was given to you directly
by my Father in heaven."

MATTHEW 16:15-17

A missionary
was translating the Bible into Songhai.
Unable to find a word for "to believe,"
he asked a native how to translate it.
The native thought a second and said,
"It means to hear with the heart."
That's a perfect translation. For God
doesn't speak with a physical voice,
but with a spiritual voice—
one that can be heard by the heart alone.
This is what Jesus meant
when he said to Peter, "This truth . . .
was given to you directly by my Father."

How can I learn to listen with my heart?

We can't always trust
what we hear with our ears,
but we can always trust
what we hear with our heart.

FRIDAY
Ordinary Time
Week 18 _____

Jesus said to his disciples,
"If anyone wants to come with me,
he must forget himself,
carry his cross, and follow me."

MATTHEW 16:24

Years ago, the *London Times*
carried this tiny advertisement:
"Men wanted for hazardous journey.
Small wages, bitter cold,
long months of complete darkness,
constant danger, safe return doubtful.
Honor and recognition
in case of success."
That ad drew over 5,000 applicants.
From these applicants
Sir Ernest Shackleton picked 27 men
to explore the South Pole with him.
Eventually the entire crew
completed their exploration and
returned home to honor and recognition.

Jesus knew the power of challenge also.
His first disciples rose to the challenge,
and people are still rising to it.
What makes me want to accept
the challenge of Jesus?

Give the best you have
to the highest you know—and do it now.
RALPH W. SOCKMAN

SATURDAY
Ordinary Time
Week 18

*[One day Jesus' disciples tried to expel
a demon from someone, but couldn't.
Later they asked Jesus why they failed.]
He said to them,
"Because of your little faith. . . .
If you have faith
the size of a mustard seed . . . .
nothing will be impossible for you."*

MATTHEW 17:20 (NRSV)

In 1961 an arsonist was sentenced
to twelve years in the state prison
at Stillwater, Minnesota.
When he was released in 1973,
he found it hard
to adjust to the changes in society
that had taken place during those years.
He probably would have drifted
back into prison
had it not been for a college teacher
who believed in him and helped him.
"That person's faith," he said,
"healed and saved me."

What might I do to increase my faith
in God and in people?

*The well of Providence is deep.
It's the buckets we bring to it
that are small.*

MARY WEBB

SUNDAY
Ordinary Time
Week 19 _____

[After feeding the crowd miraculously,]
Jesus made the disciples
get into the boat and go on ahead
to the other side of the lake,
while he sent the people away.
After sending the people away,
he went up a hill by himself to pray.

MATTHEW 14:22-23

Nobel Prize winner Dr. Alexis Carrel
wrote a book called *Man, the Unknown.*
In it, he makes this striking statement:
"Prayer
is the most powerful form of energy
we can generate. . . .
The influence of prayer
on the human mind and body is
as demonstrable as secreting glands. . . .
Only in prayer do we achieve
that complete and harmonious assembly
of body, mind, and spirit
which gives the frail human reed
its unshakable strength."

What is one effect
that regular prayer has had on my life?

Much prayer, much power!
Little prayer, little power!
No prayer, no power!

ANONYMOUS

MONDAY
Ordinary Time
Week 19

*[One day Jesus said,] "The Son of Man
is about to be handed over to men
who will kill him; but three days later
he will be raised to life."
The disciples became very sad.*

MATTHEW 17:22-23

In the 1960s two famous stage plays
dealt with Jesus:
Jesus Christ Superstar and *Godspell.*
Both had superb staging and music,
but they had one significant difference.
Superstar ended with Jesus' death;
Godspell ended with Jesus' resurrection,
portrayed by the disciples
carrying Jesus' body on their shoulders
down the center aisle of the theater,
singing joyously, "Long Live God!"

In today's reading, the disciples
"became very sad" because they did
what *Jesus Christ Superstar* did.
They separated
Jesus' death from his resurrection.

How do I, perhaps, tend to separate
Jesus' death and resurrection in life?

*We die daily. Happy those
who daily come to life as well.*

GEORGE MACDONALD

TUESDAY
Ordinary Time
Week 19

Jesus called a child,
had him stand in front of them, and said,
"I assure you that unless you change
and become like children, you will
never enter the Kingdom of heaven."

MATTHEW 18:2-3

Novelist John Updike says
that when we lose touch with children,
we stop being human and become
machines for eating and making money.
A child's trust speaks of the trust
that Jesus said we should have
in our heavenly Father.
A child's wonder at the world
speaks to us of the wonder
that we should have
for our Father's universe.
Finally, a child's response to our love
speaks to us of the response
we should make to God's love for us.

What is one thing in nature
that still ignites my wonder
and raises my mind and heart to God?

Nature has perfections in order to show
that she is the image of God;
and defects to show
that she is only his image.

BLAISE PASCAL

*[Jesus said,] "Where two or three
come together in my name,
I am there with them."*

MATTHEW 18:20

The telephone rang
in a famous Washington, D.C., church.
The caller asked,
"Do you expect the president
to be at services on Sunday?"
The pastor replied,
"I'm not sure of the president's plans,
but I know Jesus intends to be there."
We sometimes forget that each time
we gather in Jesus' name, he is with us.
It is this great mystery that transpires
each time we gather in the Lord's name
to share the word and supper of the Lord.

Can I recall a time
when I seemed to experience
the Lord's presence in a special way
when gathered with others
in the Lord's name?

*The difference between listening
to a radio sermon and going to church . . .
is almost the difference between
calling your girl on the telephone
and spending the evening with her.*

L. GENE STEWART

THURSDAY
Ordinary Time
Week 19 _____

Peter came to Jesus and asked,
"Lord, if my brother keeps on sinning
against me, how many times
do I have to forgive him? Seven times?"
"No, not seven times," answered Jesus,
"but seventy times seven."

MATTHEW 18:21-22

A woman was referred to a specialist
by her doctor.
When the specialist checked her,
he found her condition vastly improved.
The woman's doctor was stunned.
He asked her, "Did anything unusual
take place since I last saw you?"
"Yes," she said, "I made up with someone
with whom I had been feuding for years."
Modern medicine is starting to document
what the Bible seems to imply:
there's often a connection
between sin and illness (LUKE 5:17-20).

Can I recall a time when refusing
to forgive another person
affected my health?

Our feelings about ourselves
and others . . . may have more to do
with how often we get sick, than our genes,
chemistry, diet, or environment.

BRUCE LARSON

And God said . . .
"A man will leave his father and mother
and unite with his wife,
and the two will become one."

MATTHEW 19:5

A young mother with small children
wrote to Ann Landers.
Her husband had done something stupid
and she had separated from him.
Ann wrote back, "Don't be stubborn
and proud. Take him back.
I promise you won't regret it."
Years later another woman wrote to Ann.
She had just buried her husband.
Eight years earlier she left her husband,
but returned to him because of the reply
that Ann had given the young mother.
She thanked Ann for her advice,
saying their last eight years together
were the happiest of their married life.

What is one way that I could improve
my relationship with a spouse or a friend
with whom I am having problems?

When one door of happiness closes,
another one opens; but we look so long
at the closed door that we do not see
the one which has been opened for us.

HELEN KELLER

SATURDAY
Ordinary Time
Week 19

*[The disciples began to scold the people
for bringing children to Jesus to bless.
Jesus intervened and said,]
"Let the children come to me
and do not stop them."*

MATTHEW 19:14

Children, more than anyone else,
need assurance that they are loved.
They need to feel
the touch of an adult hand,
the warmth of an adult cheek,
the embrace of adult arms.
"Love locked in our hearts
doesn't reach them;
it is like a letter written
and not sent. . . .
[Children] must hear:
I love you.
I am proud of you.
I am glad you are here."

JANE LINDSTROM

How warm and reassuring am I
in my dealings with other people,
especially children and my family?

*The scars left from the child's defeat
in the fight against irrational authority
are at the bottom of every neurosis.*

ERICH FROMM

[A woman, who was not a Jew,
was calling to Jesus to heal her child.
The disciples said to Jesus,]
"Send her away! She is following us
and making all this noise!"
[After testing the woman, Jesus said,]
"You are a woman of great faith!
What you want will be done for you."
And at that very moment
her daughter was healed.

MATTHEW 15:23, 28

USA Today showed a striking photo
of a legless man,
his arms upstretched in a "V for victory" sign.
It was Bob Wieland, who lost his legs
in a land-mine explosion.
He had just finished the 26.2 mile
New York City Marathon on his hands.
It took him five days, but he did it.

Bob's dogged spirit reflects
the woman's dogged spirit in the Bible.
In both cases it paid off dramatically.
How ready am I to confront the odds
to achieve something I esteem?

What counts is not necessarily
the size of the dog in the fight—
it's the size of the fight in the dog.

DWIGHT D. EISENHOWER

MONDAY
Ordinary Time
Week 20

*[Jesus said to a young man
who kept the commandments faithfully,]
"To be perfect, go and sell all you have
and give the money to the poor . . . ;
then come and follow me."
When the young man heard this,
he went away sad, because he was very rich.*

MATTHEW 19:21-22

An update of that story reads:
"A high school athlete asked Jesus,
'What must I do to be your follower?'
Jesus said, 'Respect your teammates,
obey your coach, work hard, play fair.'
The athlete said, 'I do all this now.'
Jesus said, 'If you want to be perfect,
forget about player popularity and
use your talent to coach unfortunate kids
who have no one to teach or guide them.'
When the young athlete heard this,
he went away sad."

How do I know if God is calling me
to a special kind of Christian perfection?

*The happiest people in the world
are those who have found the life task
to which they have been called. . . .
[And the unhappiest] are those
who have not even begun to search.*

ROBERT C. LESLIE

TUESDAY
Ordinary Time
Week 20

[Jesus said,] "Everyone who has left houses
or brothers or sisters or father
or mother . . . for my sake,
will receive a hundred times more
and will be given eternal life."

MATTHEW 19:29

Stephen Doyle proposes a case.
Suppose a teacher told her class,
"I am your teacher.
You must put me before your parents.
You must be ready and willing
to follow me without any questions!"
No teacher
has a right to make such a demand.
That's why we miss the point
if we think of Jesus only as a teacher.
He's infinitely more; he's the Son of God.

What keeps me from grasping
more fully who Jesus really is?

When a Harvard University president
was asked to name
the fundamental quality of leadership,
he replied, "The capacity to inflict pain."
That is a blunt way of saying
that leadership requires courage
to speak the unvarnished truth,
however unpopular it may be.

H. B. WALKER, *Days Demanding Courage*

WEDNESDAY
Ordinary Time
Week 20 _____

*[Jesus told a parable about an employer
who went out at five different times
during the day to hire workers.
At day's end he paid all workers
a full day's wage, even the latecomers.
When some workers complained,
the owner asked,]* " *'Don't I have the right
to do as I wish with my own money?
Or are you jealous because I am generous?'* "

MATTHEW 20:15

Poor people lived from day to day
in Jesus' time. If a man didn't work today,
his family didn't eat tomorrow.
Had the early workers not learned
that the employer paid all the workers
a full day's wage,
they would have gone home joyful.
The latecomers stand for repentant sinners.
The early workers stand for those Pharisees
who resented sinners entering the Kingdom
of God late and getting the same reward.

How prone am I to resent or envy
the good fortune of others?

*In a consumer society there are . . .
two kinds of slaves:
the prisoners of addiction and
the prisoners of envy.*

IVAN ILLICH

THURSDAY
Ordinary Time
Week 20

*[Jesus told this parable to illustrate
what the Kingdom of heaven was like.
A king held a wedding feast for his son.
When many invited guests didn't show,
he opened the doors to "other" guests.
One of these guests came]
not wearing wedding clothes. . . .
Then the king told the servants . . .
["Expel and punish this person!"]*

MATTHEW 22:11,13

The "invited" guests are the Jews.
The "other" guests are the Gentiles.
The Gentiles' belated invitation, however,
doesn't exempt them
from basic banquet etiquette.
To accept an invitation means, also,
to come properly dressed.
We have accepted God's invitation
to the wedding banquet of heaven.
We must come to it "dressed" properly—
in garments of love and gratitude.

How loving and grateful am I to God?
What is one concrete way
I show this love and gratitude?

*O Thou who has given us so much,
mercifully grant us one thing more—
a grateful heart.*

GEORGE HERBERT

FRIDAY
Ordinary Time
Week 20 _____

[When someone asked Jesus
which was the greatest commandment,]
Jesus answered, " 'Love the Lord your God
with all your heart, with all your soul,
and with all your mind.' "

MATTHEW 22:37

Austrian psychologist Viktor Frankl
was imprisoned by the Nazis
during World War II.
The first thing they did was to take
his good clothes and give him
the rags of a dead prisoner.
In the pocket of the rags
Frankl found a copy of the Shema Israel,
which Jesus refers to in today's reading:
"Israel, remember this!
The LORD—and the LORD alone—
is our God. Love the LORD your God
with all your heart, with all your soul,
and with all your strength" (DEUT. 6:4-5).
That tattered copy of the Shema Israel
sustained him powerfully
in the dark days of his imprisonment.

What prayer sustains me in dark days?

A good prayer, though often used,
is still fresh and fair
in the eyes and ears of heaven.

THOMAS FULLER

*[Jesus said,] "The greatest among you
will be your servant. . . .
All who humble themselves
will be exalted."*

MATTHEW 23:11–12 (NRSV)

In the early 1980s
attorney Michael Minton did a study
of the service of mothers to their families.
He began by listing the functions
mothers perform, for example,
dietician, chauffeur, budget manager.
Next, he assigned a monetary value
to each of these functions.
Finally, he added up all the values.
The total was about $40,000 a year.
Minton's study gives us
a new appreciation of the service
mothers render to those around them.
According to Jesus' evaluation,
they rank among the "greatest" of us all.

What is one way I might better show
my appreciation to mothers?

*I'm going your way,
so let us go hand in hand. . . .
For soon death, the kind old nurse,
will come back and rock us all to sleep.
Let us help one another while we may.*

WILLIAM MORRIS

SUNDAY
Ordinary Time
Week 21 _____

[One day Jesus asked his disciples,]
"Who do you say I am?"
Simon Peter answered,
"You are the Messiah,
the Son of the living God."

MATTHEW 16:15-16

A poem describes six blind people
wondering what an elephant looks like.
One feels the animal's side and says,
"It looks like a wall."
Another feels the elephant's leg and says,
"It looks like a tree trunk"; and so on.
Some people say, "When it comes to God,
the various religions of the world
are like the blind people in the poem.
Each is partly in the right;
each is partly in the wrong."

What convinces me that Christianity
is different from other religions
and is right about God?

Muhammad said he was a sinner.
Buddha said he wasn't God.
Jesus said, "Whoever has seen me
has seen the Father" (JOHN 14:9).
If Jesus was who he said he was,
then Christianity does, indeed, possess
a privileged, personal knowledge
of God and God's will.

MONDAY
Ordinary Time
Week 21

[Jesus said,] "How terrible for you,
teachers of the Law and Pharisees! . . . .
You lock the door to the
Kingdom of heaven in people's faces,
but you yourselves don't go in,
nor do you allow in those
who are trying to enter!"

MATTHEW 23:13

Jesus had a "stormy north side."
We see it in today's reading.
Certain Jewish leaders had turned
religion into a cruel game of rules.
Worse yet, they were forcing their game
on illiterate, simple people.
Jesus castigates these leaders.
Religion is not a game of rules—
the creation of a cruel God.
It is an expression of love—
the creation of a compassionate God.

Saint Augustine said,
"Love God and do what you will."
What important point is he making?

When I die,
God won't measure my head
to see how clever I was.
God will measure my heart
to see how loving I was.

ANONYMOUS

TUESDAY
Ordinary Time
Week 21

[Jesus said,] "How terrible for you,
teachers of the Law and Pharisees!
You hypocrites! You give to God
one tenth even of the seasoning herbs, . . .
but you neglect to obey
the really important teachings
of the Law, such as
justice and mercy and honesty. . . .
You strain a fly out of your drink,
but swallow a camel!"

MATTHEW 23:23-24

Ancient peoples poured liquids through
a cloth to strain out foreign particles
like dead flies or insects.
Picture these same people
eating a dung-smeared camel.
Jesus uses this ridiculous image
to show the teachers and Pharisees
how inconsistent they are.
They give one-tenth of their wealth
to the Temple,
but treat people with contempt.

To what extent do I occasionally
strain out flies and swallow camels
in the practice of my faith? How?

A test of worship is how sensitive
it makes me to needs of those around me.

ANONYMOUS

WEDNESDAY
Ordinary Time
Week 21

[Jesus said to the Pharisees
and the teachers of the Law,]
"You hypocrites!
You are like whitewashed tombs,
which look fine on the outside
but are full of bones
and decaying corpses on the inside."

MATTHEW 23:27

Ancient Jews buried their dead
in tombs above ground.
The outside of these tombs
was whitewashed to look nice.
The inside, however,
was filled with rotting flesh.
Jesus used this image to give
teachers of the Law and Pharisees
a picture of themselves.
On the outside, they looked nice,
appearing to be good and holy.
On the inside, however,
they were neither good nor holy.

What is one way
that my outer actions are not
a faithful reflection of my inner state?
When is this bad? Good?

When we try to make an impression,
that's exactly the impression we make.

ANONYMOUS

THURSDAY
Ordinary Time
Week 21 _____

[Jesus warned his followers,]
"The Son of Man will come at an hour
when you are not expecting him."

MATTHEW 24:44

Three apprentice devils
were preparing to go up to earth
for some on-the-job training.
Their teacher asked each one,
"What technique do you plan to use
to get people to sin?"
The first devil said, "I plan to use
the *classical* approach. I'll tell people,
'There is no God, so sin all you want.'"
The second devil said, "I plan to use
the *intellectual* approach. I'll tell them,
'There's no hell, so sin all you want.'"
The third devil said, "I plan to use
a more *subtle* approach. I'll tell them,
'There's no hurry, so sin all you want.
You can repent and be good later.'"

What is one thing I should change,
but keep putting off?

A rabbi told a student,
"Everything can teach us something."
The student asked,
"What can a train teach us?"
The rabbi said, "That one minute
can cause us to miss everything."

[Jesus told the following parable.
Ten girls were waiting for the groom
to arrive at the bride's house.
Night fell, and the groom didn't show.
The girls fell asleep. The result?
Half of the girls missed his coming.]
Jesus concluded, "Watch out, then,
because you do not know the day
or the hour [of the Son of Man's coming]."

MATTHEW 25:13

Ancient weddings lasted for days.
A highpoint was the arrival of the groom
at the bride's house,
where bridesmaids met him joyfully.
Ancient literature says that grooms
sometimes delayed their arrival—
waiting even until midnight—
to catch the bridesmaids off guard.
Jesus used this image
to teach people about his final coming.
It will catch many people off guard.
As a result they will not be prepared.

If the Second Coming of Jesus
were to take place an hour from now,
what is one way that I would be
caught off guard and not prepared?

Eternity is the ocean; time is the wave.

MAURICE MAETERLINCK

314

*[A master gave money
to three servants to invest.
The two who were given the most money
turned a profit and were rewarded.
The third, who was given less money,
turned no profit. So the master said
to the other servants,] "Now, take
the money away from him and . . .
throw him outside in the darkness."*

MATTHEW 25:28,30

A little girl returned home
after visiting the family of a classmate
who had died suddenly.
Her father was annoyed, saying,
"Why did you go over there at this time?"
The child said, "To console her mother."
Her father said, "But what could you do?"
"Nothing," said the child,
"so I sat in her lap and cried with her."

The story of the child and Jesus' parable
invite me to ask myself,
To what extent
do I end up doing next to nothing
to advance God's Kingdom
because I feel I can do so little?

*Faithfulness in little things
is a big thing.*

SAINT JOHN CHRYSOSTOM

315

[Jesus said to his disciples,]
"I must . . . be put to death,
but three days later I will be raised."

MATTHEW 16:21

A woods surrounds a retreat house
in Barrington, Illinois.
Tucked away among the trees
is a life-sized stone crucifix.
It is especially striking at night,
because it is floodlighted dramatically.
It is even more striking on rainy nights,
because then water trickles down
the face and the body of Jesus.
One rainy night
a retreatant came upon the crucifix
and was deeply moved.
Going up to it and touching it,
the retreatant prayed for a long time.
Later, the retreatant said, "I touched
only the cross because I wasn't worthy
to touch the body of Jesus."

The retreatant's story invites me
to ask: Why did Jesus die as he did?

The cross is
a sign, an invitation, and a revelation:
a sign of Jesus' love,
an invitation to love as Jesus loved,
a revelation that love entails suffering.

MONDAY
Ordinary Time
Week 22 _____

[Jesus said to the people,]
"There were many widows in Israel. . . .
Yet Elijah was not sent
to anyone in Israel, but only
to the widow . . . in Zarephath. . . .
And there were many people
suffering from a dreaded skin disease
who lived in Israel
during the time of the prophet Elisha;
yet not one of them was healed,
but only Naaman the Syrian."
When the people . . . heard this,
they were filled with anger.

LUKE 4:25–28

Jesus was simply speaking the truth.
What he said was verifiable.
But his audience resented the fact
that he was praising Gentiles—non-Jews.
It was like eulogizing a Democrat
at a Republican convention.
People often find the truth disturbing.
They don't want to hear it.

To what extent do I, sometimes,
let the desire to be liked by others
keep me from speaking out when I should?

A lie travels round the world
while truth is putting on her boots.

CHARLES SPURGEON

*[While Jesus was preaching one day,
an evil spirit in a man shouted,]*
"I know who you are:
you are God's holy messenger!"
Jesus ordered the spirit,
"Be quiet and come out of the man!"
The demon . . . went out of him. . . .
The report about Jesus
spread everywhere.   LUKE 4:34-36

A TV program dealt with
the making of the Superman films.
One member of the film crew
was outraged to hear how much money
Marlon Brando got for a brief appearance
in one of the films.
But the outrage turned to praise
when the crew member saw, firsthand,
Brando's power to move an audience.
Jesus possessed a similar power—
only infinitely greater—
to move the human heart and
to expel evil from it.

What is one evil tendency in my heart
that I would like Jesus to heal—or to expel?

Tell everyone who is discouraged . . .
"God is coming to your rescue."
          ISAIAH 35:4

WEDNESDAY
Ordinary Time
Week 22 _____

At daybreak Jesus left the town
and went off to a lonely place [to pray].

LUKE 4:42

Catherine de Hueck Doherty
came to Canada as a Russian refugee.
After her husband died,
she arranged for her son's education,
sold everything, and went to live
in the slums of Toronto.
There she served society's outcasts.
Later she wrote a book called *Poustinia.*
Poustinia is Russian for "desert."
But it means more than a physical place.
It means an isolated place
where a person can pray in solitude
without interruption.
Like Jesus, Catherine de Hueck Doherty
sought solitude to pray and to reflect.

The modern poet Carl Sandburg said,
"One of the greatest necessities
in America
is to discover creative solititude."
His remark makes me ask,
What did Sandburg have in mind
when he said this?

Solitude shows us what we should be;
society shows us what we are.

JOSH BILLINGS

THURSDAY
Ordinary Time
Week 22

[One day Jesus told his disciples
to lower their fishing nets for a catch.
Peter was skeptical, but said,]
"If you say so, I will let down the nets."
They let them down
and caught such a large number of fish
that the nets were about to break.

LUKE 5:5-6

A sign on the shore of Lake Galilee
quotes Peter's words in today's reading.
The sign goes on to say:
"The words and deeds of Jesus
are not actions of the distant past.
Jesus is still looking for men and women
who are prepared
to take risks at his word
because they trust him utterly."
Peter's trust in Jesus,
and the catch of fish that followed,
were recorded not merely to inspire us
but to invite us to imitate Peter.

Is there some risk, perhaps,
that Jesus may be inviting me
to take for him at this time in my life?

The greatest mistake is to do nothing
because you can do only a little.
Do what you can.

SYDNEY SMITH (slightly adapted)

FRIDAY
Ordinary Time
Week 22 _____

[Someone asked Jesus why his disciples
did not fast.] Jesus answered,
"Do you think you can make the guests
at a wedding party go without food
as long as the bridegroom is with them?"

LUKE 5:34

Ancient Greeks fasted
to achieve mental sharpness.
American Indians fasted
to be able to demonstrate courage.
Russian icon artists fasted
to paint more beautifully.
Jews fasted to hasten the coming
of God's Kingdom.
Jesus' reply to the person's question
indicates that the reason for fasting
is ended. God's Kingdom is at hand.
The Messiah has come.

Jesus said the day would come, however,
when his disciples would fast again
(LUKE 5:35). How open am I to fasting
occasionally for a religious motive,
like seeking closer union with Jesus?

How far I am in tune
with the divine essence I do not know.
But I know that the fast has made
the passion for such a state intenser.

MOHANDAS GANDHI, after a long fast

SATURDAY
Ordinary Time
Week 22

[Some Pharisees complained when they saw
Jesus' disciples picking grain
off stalks of wheat on the Sabbath
and eating it. Jesus reminded them
that David and his men did not hesitate
to do something similar when hungry.]
Jesus concluded,
"The Son of Man is Lord of the Sabbath."

LUKE 6:5

Some Jewish soldiers were in battle
when the Sabbath dawned.
They hid in a cave rather than break
the Sabbath by fighting.
The enemy found them and slayed them
without their lifting a hand in defense.
Respect for law had a flip side.
Some Jews gave higher priority
to the letter of the law than to its spirit.
One rabbi went so far as to hold
that if a wall toppled on a person,
it would be breaking the Sabbath
to remove the rubble from the person.

What is one way that I tend to worship
more according to the letter of the law
than according to its spirit? Why?

Observance without reason
is not worship, but idolatry.
ANONYMOUS

SUNDAY
Ordinary Time
Week 23 _____

[Jesus said,]
"Where two or three come together
in my name, I am there with them."

MATTHEW 18:20

George Anderson was a chaplain
at New York's Riker's Island prison.
One night he was praying
with a small group of prisoners
over the story of the Good Samaritan.
A mentally disturbed prisoner, Richard,
was present for the first time.
The room was cold,
and Richard was wrapped in two blankets.
The prisoner opposite him was shivering.
At one point
while the group was praying in silence,
Richard suddenly got up,
walked over to the shivering man,
and put a blanket around him.
Richard's silent action witnessed
not only to Jesus' *words* to us
about loving others,
but also to Jesus' *presence* among us
when we gather in his name.

Can I recall a time when I felt moved
by Jesus' *words* or his *presence* in a group?

Wherever you see another, there I am.

RABBINICAL SAYING

MONDAY
Ordinary Time
Week 23

*[A man with a paralyzed hand
came into the synagogue on the Sabbath.
Jesus' opponents watched to see
if Jesus would heal on the Sabbath.
Jesus told the man,]*
*"Stretch out your hand." He did so,
and his hand became well again.*

LUKE 6:10

One day Jesus appeared to an old monk.
At the very instant that Jesus appeared,
the bell rang, calling the monk
to feed the poor at the monastery gate.
The monk was torn
between Jesus and feeding the poor.
Then he decided to turn his back
on his vision of Jesus and feed the poor.
When the monk returned,
Jesus was still there and said to him,
"Had you not gone to feed the poor,
I would not have stayed."
The story of the old monk and today's gospel
make the same point: helping the needy
takes priority over worship and prayer.

What kind of priority do I put
on helping the needy? Why?

*Those who close their ears to the needy
will themselves cry and not be heard.*
OLD HEBREW PROVERB

TUESDAY
Ordinary Time
Week 23 ⎯⎯⎯⎯⎯⎯⎯⎯

*Jesus went up a hill to pray
and spent the whole night there
praying to God.*   LUKE 6:12

A shabbily dressed man was walking
along a few yards ahead of a woman.
As she approached, she could hear him
talking out loud to himself, saying:
"What do you think Jesus
would say about this?
You know darn well what he'd say!
So what are you going to do?
Well, you'd better do something,
and you'd better do it soon!"
What struck the woman
was that the man was stone sober.
Moreover, he didn't care who heard him.
She envied him.

Speaking out loud in prayer isn't new.
It goes back to biblical times.
It heightens reality and
gives a greater intensity to our prayer.
Did I ever pray out loud? When and why?
Have I considered praying out loud,
occasionally, in my daily prayer?

*Scream at God if that is the only thing
that will get results.*

BRENDAN FRANCIS

WEDNESDAY
Ordinary Time
Week 23

[Jesus said,]
"Happy are you when people hate you . . .
because of the Son of Man! Be glad . . .
and dance for joy, because a great reward
is kept for you in heaven."

LUKE 6:22-23

Kim Chi Ha is a South Korean poet.
He was sentenced to life imprisonment
for writing several poems protesting
his government's treatment of the poor.
In the midst of his ordeal,
Kim never lost his joy or sense of humor.
When an angry judge added seven years
to his sentence, he joked to his mother,
"I must stay in prison
seven more years after I die."
Kim's mother supports her son totally,
saying, "Jesus was always for the poor.
We, too, if we are to be his followers,
must be for the poor and oppressed."

Kim's mother's support of her son's work
invites me to inventory my own support
of people and causes
involving the fundamental principles
of human rights and justice.

A people that values its privileges
above its principles soon loses both.

DWIGHT D. EISENHOWER

THURSDAY
Ordinary Time
Week 23 _____

[Jesus said,]
"Do not judge others,
and God will not judge you;
do not condemn others,
and God will not condemn you."

LUKE 6:37

A teacher said to her students,
"Tonight I want you to go home and
compliment your mother for something."
The next day
the students reported on the assignment.
One boy said, "It was a total disaster!"
He explained why, saying:
"After supper I told my mother,
'Gee, Mom, that was a great meal.'
She looked at me kind of funny and said,
'What are you setting me up for?'
'Nothing,' I said, 'It was really good!'
She said, 'Well, if it was so good,
show your appreciation. Do the dishes.'"
The boy meant the compliment,
but his mother misjudged him.

How prone am I to jump to conclusions
or to say things too hastily
before thinking them through?

Once the toothpaste is out of the tube,
it's hard to get it back again.

H. R. HALDEMAN

[Jesus said,]
"One blind man cannot lead another one;
if he does, both will fall into a ditch."

LUKE 6:39

Before the era of radio and TV,
a small-town telephone operator
used to get a daily call
requesting the exact time.
She always gave it with confidence,
because she set her watch daily
when the town's only factory
sounded its whistle.
One day her watch stopped.
When the daily call came,
she explained that she was waiting
for the factory whistle.
She told the caller that she used it
to set her watch each day.
There was a silence. Then the caller said,
"This is the factory. We call you each day
for the exact time to sound our whistle."

When it comes to right and wrong,
do we follow the information of others,
who may be as blind as we are?
Or do we follow the "light of the world"?

If you think education is expensive,
try ignorance.

DEREK BOK

SATURDAY
Ordinary Time
Week 23 _____

[Jesus said,]
"Anyone who hears my words
and does not obey them
is like a man who built his house
without laying a foundation;
when the flood hit that house it fell . . .
and what a terrible crash that was!"

LUKE 6:49

A *Peanuts* cartoon shows Linus
building sand castles on a beach.
Soon the beach is covered with them.
Then a heavy rainstorm hits
and washes them all into the sea.
Linus looks on in total disbelief.

Linus would have no trouble
grasping Jesus' point in today's gospel.
Listening to God's word
without implementing it
is like building sand castles on a beach
before a rainstorm.
What is one word/teaching of Jesus
that I am not sure how to implement?

Lord, help us
not only to hear your word
but to implement it,
not only to love your word but to live it,
not only to profess our faith
but to practice it.

SUNDAY
Ordinary Time
Week 24

Peter came to Jesus and asked,
"Lord, if my brother
keeps on sinning against me,
how many times
do I have to forgive him? Seven times?"
"No, not seven times," answered Jesus,
"but seventy times seven."

MATTHEW 18:21-22

Whenever we forgive from the heart,
we build a bridge
over which we must pass
on our way from earth to heaven.
For each of us is a sinner.
And the only way we can pass
from earth to heaven
is over the bridge of God's forgiveness.
"If you forgive others . . . ," Jesus said,
"your Father in heaven
will also forgive you" (MATTHEW 6:14).
In other words,
the surest insurance policy
against the loss of heaven
is to forgive others from the heart.

Jesus' words invite me
to recall someone who has hurt me
and to consciously forgive that person now.

To err is human, to forgive divine.
ALEXANDER POPE

MONDAY
Ordinary Time
Week 24

*[A Roman officer
asked Jesus to cure his servant, saying,]
"I do not deserve to have you come
into my house. . . . Just give the order,
and my servant will get well." . . .
Jesus was surprised . . .
and said to the crowd following him,
"I have never found faith like this,
not even in Israel!"*

LUKE 7:6-7, 9

Faith is a gift from God.
We might compare it
to someone's gift of seed to a farmer.
He can bring only one sack to be filled,
or he can bring 100 sacks.
God proportions God's gifts
to our readiness to receive them.
And when the farmer receives the seed,
he can plant it and cultivate it.
Or he can store it and ignore it.
The same option is open to us
when it comes to God's gift of faith.

This raises an important question:
How am I cultivating my faith?

*I give you the end of a Golden String.
Only wind it into a ball—
It will lead you to heaven's gate.*

WILLIAM BLAKE

*[The funeral of a widow's only son
moved Jesus. Touching the coffin,
he said,] "Young man! Get up. . . !
The dead man sat up and began to talk,
and Jesus gave him back to his mother.*

LUKE 7:14-15

Network television carried the story
of Alfredo, a 12-year-old Mexican boy.
He lost his entire family in a fire,
which also disfigured his face horribly.
Incredibly, no one took Alfredo in,
and he ended up living on the streets.
One day he stumbled upon an orphanage,
sought admission, and was accepted.
That night the orphanage celebrated
Alfredo's arrival. Amidst the festivities,
the camera cut to Alfredo's face.
For the first time since the fire,
it glowed with a beautiful smile.
A dead Alfredo was raised to new life.
Once again he had a family.

How sensitive am I to people
who suffer misfortune?
Is there such a person in my life right now?

*We can live forty days without food,
eight minutes without air,
but about one second without hope.*

HAL LINDSAY (slightly adapted)

WEDNESDAY
Ordinary Time
Week 24 ⎯⎯⎯⎯⎯⎯⎯⎯

*[Jesus compared some people to children
of whom their playmates said,]*
" 'We played wedding music for you,
but you wouldn't dance! We sang
funeral songs, but you wouldn't cry!'
John the Baptist came,
and he fasted and drank no wine,
and you said, 'He has a demon in him!'
The Son of Man came,
and he ate and drank, and you said,
'Look at this . . . wine-drinker.' "

LUKE 7:32-34

In Jesus' day, children played games
like "funeral" and "wedding."
One child played a dead person,
and the others cried and wailed.
Two children played newlyweds,
and the others sang and danced.
Sometimes, however, when the children
didn't get their way, they quit playing.
Jesus used this image
to describe certain people of his day.
They behaved like children.

How do I react
when things don't go my way? Why?

*The discontented child cries
for toasted snow.*

ARAB PROVERB

[Jesus told Simon the Pharisee
about a person who forgave two people
debts of different amounts.
One debt was small; the other, large.
Then Jesus asked Simon,]
"Which one, then, will love him more?"
"I suppose," answered Simon, ". . .
the one who was forgiven more."
"You are right," said Jesus.

LUKE 7:42-43

A member of Alcoholics Anonymous said:
"I wish everyone
could become alcoholic for a short time.
If they did, we'd have a different world.
When people hit bottom, they change.
If they tended to be proud,
they become much more humble.
And if they tended to be judgmental,
they become much more tolerant,
because you know from bitter experience
how easy it is to fall."

These words prompt me to ask:
What kind of tendency do I have
to be proud and judgmental?
Concerning what things?

No human being is too big to be humble,
but some human beings are too small.

ANONYMOUS

FRIDAY
Ordinary Time
Week 24 _____

Jesus traveled through towns and villages,
preaching the Good News
about the Kingdom of God.
The twelve disciples went with him,
and so did some women . . .
who used their own resources
to help Jesus and his disciples.

LUKE 8:1-3

A least-watched moment of TV
is when the commercial runs.
But there's another moment
that receives far less attention yet:
when the credits of the program run.
Yet if it weren't for the people
whose names roll across the screen
at that moment,
we wouldn't have any programs at all.
Today's reading
is like the "credit" moment on TV.
We are introduced to some of the people
who worked behind the scenes
to help Jesus fund his preaching mission.

How content am I to play
a behind-the-scenes role in God's work,
such as funding it anonymously?

Money is a terrible master
but an excellent servant.

P. T. BARNUM

*[After telling the Parable of the Sower,
Jesus said to his disciples,]*
*"The seeds that fell among thorn bushes
stand for those who hear [God's word];
but the worries . . . of this life . . .
choke them, and their fruit never ripens."*

LUKE 8:14

A teacher read the Parable of the Sower.
Then she asked her students
to write a paragraph
explaining what seed they were like:
the seed that fell on the footpath,
on the rock, amid thorn bushes,
or in good soil. One student wrote:
"I am like the seed that fell amid thorns.
This is because I live in a home
with an emotionally sick father.
I receive God's word in church,
but then I go home to a family argument.
This chokes God's word inside me,
and I end up losing the hope I'd built up."

How aware am I of sorrow in the lives
of people around me? Who, for instance?

*Every man has secret sorrows,
that the world knows not;
and oftentimes we call a man cold
when he is only sad.*

HENRY WADSWORTH LONGFELLOW

SUNDAY
Ordinary Time
Week 25 _____

[Jesus told a story about a farmer
who went out at different times
of the day to hire workers.
At day's end he paid all the same wage.
When some workers protested,
the farmer said,] " 'Don't I have the right
to do as I wish with my own money?
Or are you jealous
because I am generous?' "

MATTHEW 20:15

The purpose of Jesus' story
isn't to illustrate an unfair action
by an unfair owner. The opposite is true.
It's to illustrate God's generosity.
The punch line of the story
is the farmer's question:
"Are you jealous because I am generous?"
The farmer knew that if he paid
the later workers only for the time
that they actually worked,
they wouldn't have enough to buy food
for their hungry families.
So he gave them a full day's wage.

Do I tend to have tunnel vision
and see only my world—and no one else's?

The world asks, How much does he give?
Christ asks, Why does he give?

JOHN RALEIGH MOTT

MONDAY
Ordinary Time
Week 25

[Jesus said,] "Whatever is hidden away
will be brought out into the open,
and whatever is covered up
will be found and brought to light."

LUKE 8:17

A little boy asked his mother,
"Can God see me hiding in my room?"
"Yes!" said his mother.
"Can God see me hiding in my closet?"
"Yes!" said his mother.
"Can God see me when it's dark outside?"
"Yes!" said his mother.
The boy was silent for a minute.
Then he said, "I don't much like that."
Today's gospel reading reminds us
that we are accountable to God
for everything we do—
even the secret things
that evade the notice of other people.

What is one action
that I perform somewhat consistently
that I would modify drastically
if I knew it was going to be exposed
to the view of everyone?

The measure of a man's real character
is what he will do
if he knows he will never be found out.

THOMAS MACAULEY

TUESDAY
Ordinary Time
Week 25 _____

Someone said to Jesus,
"Your mother and brothers are
standing outside and want to see you."
Jesus said to them all,
"My mother and brothers are those
who hear the word of God and obey it."

LUKE 8:20-21

Humorist Will Rogers was part Indian.
One day a woman was boasting that her
ancestors came over on the *Mayflower.*
Then, turning to Will, she said,
"What about your ancestors?"
Will said, with a mischievous twinkle
in his eye, "They met the *Mayflower.*"
Someone said,
"I'm glad Jesus didn't father a family.
It saves a lot of people the trouble
of trying to trace their ancestry
back to him."
In today's reading Jesus reminds us
that the important relationship to him
is not a physical one, but a spiritual one.
And the way we build this relationship
is to hear God's word and keep it.

How close a relationship do I want
with Jesus? What am I ready to do to get it?

Recipe for having friends: be one.
ELBERT HUBBARD

WEDNESDAY
Ordinary Time
Week 25

*Jesus called the twelve disciples together
and gave them power and authority. . . .
Then he sent them out
to preach the Kingdom of God
and to heal the sick.*   LUKE 9:1-2

President Woodrow Wilson once said,
"No one can love his neighbor
on an empty stomach."
His point is an important one:
We are made up of *soul* and *body.*
To address the soul without addressing
the body is to ignore
the reality of our human makeup.
In other words, we can't talk to people
of *heavenly* things
if we don't talk to them also
of *earthly* things.
This is why Jesus told his disciples
to "preach and to heal"—
to address both people's spiritual needs
and their physical needs.

Is there anything in my life that
needs healing before I can hear preaching?

*For every talent
that poverty has stimulated,
it has blighted a hundred.*
JOHN W. GARDNER

THURSDAY
Ordinary Time
Week 25 _____

[When Herod heard the things
Jesus was doing, he said,]
"Who is this man
I hear these things about?"

LUKE 9:9

Someone asked pianist Fats Waller
for a definition of jazz. Fats replied,
"The fact you have to ask me
means that I can't tell you."
What Fats Waller said about jazz
is true also about Jesus:
If people have to ask us who Jesus is,
that means we can't tell them.

There are certain questions to which
other people cannot give us answers.
One of these is "Who is Jesus?"
The answer to this question can't come
"from any human being," only from
the "Father in heaven" (MATTHEW 16:17).
All we can do is open our hearts
to receive it. This raises a question:
What can I do to help other people
open their hearts to the Father's answer
to the question "Who is Jesus"?

Take my hand and walk along with me,
not ahead of me;
otherwise I may not follow you.

ANONYMOUS

*One day when Jesus was praying alone,
the disciples came to him. "Who do
the crowds say I am?" he asked them.*

LUKE 9:18

Every key event in Jesus' life
found him at prayer.
Consider just a few of them.
Jesus prayed at his baptism (LUKE 3:21);
before preaching and healing (MARK 1:35);
after preaching and healing (LUKE 5:16);
before picking his Apostles (LUKE 6:12);
before asking his disciples,
"Who do you say I am?" (LUKE 9:20);
before teaching his disciples
the way they should pray (LUKE 11:1);
before going to Jerusalem (LUKE 9:29);
at the Last Supper (JOHN 17:1-26);
on the Mount of Olives (LUKE 22:41);
on the cross (LUKE 23:34).

The example of Jesus at prayer—
an operative event of his life—
invites me to ask: What were some
operative moments in my life
when I prayed? With what result?

*At the judgment seat the most
embarrassing thing the believer will face
will be the smallness of his praying.*

LEONARD RAVENHILL

SATURDAY
Ordinary Time
Week 25 _____

[Jesus said,]
"Don't forget what I am about to tell you!
The Son of Man is going to be
handed over to the power of men."

LUKE 9:44

Gardening experts tell us
that certain seeds and buds must freeze
before they can sprout or bloom.
For example, Joseph W. K. Sloane says:
"Bring a bare branch of forsythia
into the house in autumn
and the buds will never open.
Bring it in in January or February
after the buds have been well frozen
and they'll bloom."
Amateurs find such talk incredible,
just as the disciples found Jesus' talk
of suffering and dying incredible.
Yet, the great mystery of faith remains:
Without suffering and death,
there can be no resurrection—
neither Jesus' nor ours.

Can I recall a time
when some personal suffering or "death"
turned out to be life-giving for me?

Christ changed the dark door of death
into a shining gate of life.

ANONYMOUS

SUNDAY
Ordinary Time
Week 26

*[Jesus told a story about a father
who said to his son,]*
*" 'Go and work in the vineyard today.'
'I don't want to,' he answered,
but later he changed his mind and went."*

MATTHEW 21:28-29

A man turned to drink.
He also turned from God and his family.
One day while walking along,
repenting how his life turned out,
he saw a bent, rusty nail in the gutter.
It reminded him of himself and his life.
So he picked it up and took it home.
Placing the nail on an anvil, he began
to straighten it out and clean it up.
An hour later, it looked almost new again.
Then it occurred to him.
He could straighten out and clean up
his own life in the same way.
That thought triggered his conversion.
He turned away from drink
and back to God and to his family.
Today, he keeps that nail,
straightened and cleaned, in his wallet.

Was there a time when I was almost like
that bent, rusty nail? What changed me?

Who repents sin is almost innocent.
SENECA

MONDAY
Ordinary Time
Week 26 ⸻

[Placing a child at his side, Jesus said,]
"Whoever welcomes this child
in my name, welcomes me;
and whoever welcomes me,
also welcomes the one who sent me."

LUKE 9:48

Schoolchildren were cutting across
the lawn of an elderly couple,
wearing an ugly path across it.
At first this annoyed the couple;
then it angered them.
They knew something had to be done,
because the situation was destroying
their peace of mind.
The couple's solution was beautiful.
They paved the path with crushed gravel,
lined it with flowers,
and placed a bench next to it.
Then on nice days, they sat on the bench
and welcomed the children.
The children responded wonderfully.
They thanked the couple for the path,
and sat a few minutes to talk with them.

What is one situation that threatens
my peace of mind? How might I deal
with it creatively, as the couple did?

Lord, help us deal with ugly situations
in a beautiful way.

TUESDAY
Ordinary Time
Week 26

[A Samaritan village refused
to receive Jesus,] because it was clear
that he was on his way to Jerusalem.
When the disciples James and John saw this,
they said, "Lord, do you want us
to call fire down from heaven
to destroy them?"
Jesus turned and rebuked them.

LUKE 9:53–55

The heated reaction of James and John
in today's reading
shows that they have not yet mastered
this teaching of Jesus:
"Learn from me, because I am gentle
and humble of spirit" (MATTHEW 11:29).

When was one time I responded hatefully
to hateful treatment by another?
How do I deal with such treatment now?

When we hate our enemies,
we give them power over us—
power over our sleep,
power over our health,
power over our peace of mind.
Our enemies would dance for joy
if they knew
how our hatred was killing us
but not hurting them in the least.

ANONYMOUS (slightly adapted)

WEDNESDAY
Ordinary Time
Week 26 _____

[Jesus said to someone who was having
second thoughts about following him,]
"Anyone who starts to plow
and then keeps looking back
is of no use for the Kingdom of God."

LUKE 9:62

After Roger Bannister of England
broke the four-minute mile in 1954,
John Landy of Australia broke it too.
This set the stage for a dream race
between the two runners in Canada.
Landy took the lead
and led throughout the entire race.
As the two runners
headed down the final stretch,
Landy looked back briefly
to see how close Bannister was.
Bannister, who was a step off the pace,
seized the golden opportunity
and darted past Landy to win the race.

Has it ever entered my mind
to question or second-guess my decision
to follow Jesus more closely?
When? Why?

God has not called me
to be successful;
God has called me to be faithful.

MOTHER TERESA (slightly adapted)

THURSDAY
Ordinary Time
Week 26

[Jesus said to his disciples,]
"There is a large harvest,
but few workers to gather it in.
Pray to the owner of the harvest
that he will send out workers
to gather in his harvest."

LUKE 10:2

Saint Francis Xavier was born in Spain
shortly after the discovery of America.
As a student at the University of Paris,
he heard God's call to the priesthood
and later became a missionary to India.
One of his letters from India
echoes Jesus' words in today's gospel.
A portion of it reads:
"Many out here fail to become Christians
for one reason only.
There is nobody prepared to undertake
the task of teaching them about Christ.
Again and again, I have thought
of going to the universities of Europe
and crying out [for workers to help
gather in the harvest that is here]."

What is one thing that I might do to help
gather in the harvest that is in my life?

Lord, here I am.
What would you have me to do?
SAINT FRANCIS XAVIER

FRIDAY
Ordinary Time
Week 26 _____

Jesus said to his disciples,
"Whoever listens to you listens to me."

LUKE 10:16

A teacher of little children
began her class on Jesus, saying:
"Today I want to tell you about someone
you will want to meet.
This person loves you even more
than your closest friend loves you.
This person is kinder
than the kindest person you know.
This person forgives you
no matter how often you do wrong."
As the teacher continued,
she noticed a little boy in the last row
getting more and more excited.
Suddenly the little boy
could not contain himself any longer.
He blurted out excitedly,
"I know the person you're talking about!
He lives on our street."

What is one way
that my life mirrors the life of Jesus?
What is one way that it does not?

Shine through me and be so in me
that every soul I come in contact with
may feel your presence in my spirit.

JOHN HENRY NEWMAN

*[After healing and teaching many people,
the disciples, whom Jesus had sent out,]
came back in great joy.
"Lord," they said, "even the demons
obeyed us when we gave them
a command in your name!"* LUKE 10:17

An American tourist was walking down
a deserted rural road in Germany.
She came upon a shepherd grazing sheep.
A dog was diligently guarding the flock.
"What's the dog's name?" she asked.
"I'll spell it for you," said the shepherd.
"I don't like to say it out loud
unless I have something for him to do."
The shepherd's comment reminds us
of how personal and powerful a name is.
People in biblical times
held names in extra-special reverence.
So it's no surprise that Jesus' name—
when invoked—had power over demons.

How aware am I
of the power of the *name* of Jesus?
How reverently do I use Jesus' name?

*The name of Jesus is
honey for the mouth, music for the ear,
and gladness for the heart.*
SAINT BERNARD OF CLAIRVAUX

SUNDAY
Ordinary Time
Week 27 _____

[Jesus told this parable.
"An owner leased his vineyard to tenants
for a share of the crops.
At harvesttime, he sent his servants
to collect the share due him.
But the tenants abused and killed them.
Then the owner sent other servants,
but the tenants did the same thing.
Finally, the owner] sent his son. . . .
When the tenants saw the son . . .
they grabbed him . . . and killed him.
[The owner then punished the tenants.]"

MATTHEW 21:37-39

In Jesus' parable, the vineyard owner
stands for *God;* the vineyard, *Israel;*
the tenants, *Israel's leaders;*
the servants, the *prophets;* the son, *Jesus.*
The parable illustrates
both God's patience and God's justice.
God dealt patiently with Israel's leaders.
But when they refused to respond,
God passed judgment on them.

In what area of my life, especially,
has God dealt very patiently with me?

All of us must appear before Christ,
to be judged by him.
Each one will receive what he deserves.

2 CORINTHIANS 5:10

[Jesus told this parable.
"A merchant was traveling to Jericho.
A thug attacked him and left him to die.
A priest came along, but passed him by.
A Levite did the same.
Finally, a Samaritan came along,
saw the man] and took him to an inn. . . ."
Jesus concluded, ". . . Which one
of these three acted like a neighbor?"

LUKE 10:34, 36

Making a Samaritan the hero of his parable
shocked Jesus' Jewish audience.
They hated Samaritans.
Their hatred dated to Assyria's conquest
of northern Israel (Samaria) in 722 B.C.
The Samaritan survivors
intermarried with their conquerors.
This angered the other Jews.
In Jesus' day, Samaritans were banned
from the Temple and synagogues;
Samaritans, on the other hand,
banned Jews from their towns.

How ready am I to take the initiative
to tear down walls of hatred and build
bridges of love? How might I do this?

Brotherhood, once a dream and a vision,
has now become a dire necessity.

LOUIS L. MANN

TUESDAY
Ordinary Time
Week 27

[Jesus was visiting Mary and Martha.
Mary conversed with Jesus,
while Martha hurried about doing things.
Jesus said to Martha,]
"You are worried and troubled over
so many things, but just one is needed.
Mary has chosen the right thing."

LUKE 10:41-42

A father was talking with his son's teacher.
Suddenly he began to sob, saying,
"I don't live with my son, but I love him."
Regaining his composure, he explained
that his wife and family had left him.
He was a contractor
who often worked 18 hours a day.
He said, "I wanted to buy my family
all the things that I never had;
but I got so involved with my work that
I forgot about what they wanted most:
a father who was there
when they needed his love and support."

Am I so involved in working to buy things
that I'm forgetting more precious things—
things money can't buy?

Measure wealth not by the things you have,
but by the things you have
for which you would not take money.

AUTHOR UNKNOWN

One day Jesus was praying. . . .
When he had finished,
one of his disciples said to him,
"Lord, teach us to pray."

LUKE 11:1

One mistake we can make in prayer
is to confuse "faith" and "feeling."
Keith Miller did this. He says,
"I had been a spiritual sensualist,
always wanting to feel God's presence."
Of course, Keith was depressed
when he didn't feel it.
Then it hit him: If he had the *feeling*,
he didn't need the *faith*.
Keith's point is a good one.
Sometimes we feel God's presence
in prayer, but this is the exception.
If we pray to get a "warm glow,"
we risk turning prayer into
an act of sophisticated self-indulgence,
rather than into an act of selfless love.

When was one time I seemed to "feel"
God's presence—in or outside of prayer?

When we are "gifted" with an awareness
of God's presence in prayer,
we savor the "gift" until it fades.
We let God hold us and carry us,
as the sea holds and carries a vessel.

THURSDAY
Ordinary Time
Week 27 _____

[Jesus said to his disciples,]
"Ask, and you will receive."

LUKE 11:9

The film *Resurrection*
deals with the mystery of faith healing.
One scene calls for a close-up of a fly
crawling across a paralytic woman's toe.
The wiggling of her toe
is the first sign that she is being healed.
Ten flies are partially frozen to do this.
The idea is that the heat
of the camera lights will revive the fly,
enabling it to crawl on the woman's toe
and fly away on cue.
The first nine flies failed to revive
and fell lifelessly to the floor.
Ellen Burstyn, who played the woman,
thought for a moment.
Then, in the spirit of the film's message,
she prayed,
"God, please help us with this key shot."
The result?
The tenth fly performed perfectly.

How easily do I pray to God for help
in time of need?

Who pray as they ought
will endeavor to live as they pray.

AUTHOR UNKNOWN

*[Jesus warned, "When an evil spirit
is expelled from someone, leaving a void
in the person, it may try to return with]
other spirits even worse than itself. . . .
When it is all over, that person is
in worse shape than . . . at the beginning."*

LUKE 11:26

A retreatant underwent a major conversion.
She said to her retreat director,
"What do I do now?
Spiritually, I'm too weak to return
to my old haunts and my old friends.
How do I fill the void this creates?"
The woman's reasoning was correct.
If we remove something from our lives,
we must replace it with something else.
Otherwise, in a moment of temptation,
we could fall back into our old ways,
become discouraged,
and end up worse than when we started.

Have I experienced anything like this
since trying to follow Jesus
more closely in this prayer program?
How do I keep from getting discouraged
when I experience temptation—
or when I lapse into my old ways?

The only real failure is to quit.
ANONYMOUS

SATURDAY
Ordinary Time
Week 27 _____

[Someone cried out to Jesus,]
"How happy is the woman
who bore you and nursed you!"
But Jesus answered,
"Rather, how happy are those
who hear the word of God and obey it!"
LUKE 11:27-28

Two seminarians
were discussing Bible translations.
Chris said, "I like the New American.
It's more clear and easier to read."
Pat said, "I like the Jerusalem Bible.
It's more poetic and easier to pray."
A priest overheard them and said,
"I like my mother's translation.
She translates it into action.
It's more alive and easier to understand."
The mother's "translation"
is what Jesus has in mind
in today's reading.
He's talking about a "living" translation.

What is Maurice Zundel's point
when he says,
"You can understand the Bible
only on your knees"?

What I began by reading,
I must finish by acting.
HENRY DAVID THOREAU

357

[Jesus told this parable.]
"A king . . . prepared a wedding feast
for his son. He sent his servants
to tell the invited guests . . .
'Come to the wedding feast!'
But the invited guests . . .
went about their business: one went
to his farm, another to his store. . . .
[Then the king said to his servants,]
'Now go . . . and invite to the feast
as many people as you find.' . . ."
And Jesus concluded,
"Many are invited, but few are chosen."

MATTHEW 22:2-5, 9, 14

The "cast of characters"
in Jesus' parable is as follows:
the *king* is God;
the *wedding feast,* God's Kingdom;
the *first guests,* God's Chosen People;
the *latter guests,* Gentiles and sinners.

Jesus' parable invites me to ask:
To what extent am I responding
to God's invitation to the wedding feast
the way the *first* guests did:
giving priority to my business
rather than to the invitation?

Christianity is a battle—not a dream.
WENDELL PHILLIPS

MONDAY
Ordinary Time
Week 28 _____

[Jesus said to the people,]
"On the Judgment Day
the people of Nineveh will stand up
and accuse you,
because they turned from their sins
when they heard Jonah preach;
and I assure you that there is
someone here greater than Jonah!"

LUKE 11:32

God sent Jonah to warn the Ninevites
that unless they repented,
they would be punished. They repented.
Jesus compares
Jonah's preaching to the Ninevites
to his preaching to the Israelites.
But the Israelites were not as repentant
as were the Ninevites.
This explains why Jesus says,
"On the Judgment Day
the people of Nineveh will stand up
and accuse you."

How seriously
am I taking Jesus' call to repentance?
What is one concrete thing I can do
to show how serious I am in my repentance?

Of all human acts,
repentance is most divine.
THOMAS CARLYLE

TUESDAY
Ordinary Time
Week 28

*[A Pharisee was surprised that Jesus
omitted the religious washing ritual
before eating. Jesus said to him,]
"You Pharisees clean the outside
of your cup and plate, but inside
you are full of violence and evil."*

LUKE 11:39

The washing ritual began
by pouring water over the fingertips,
then over the fingers,
and finally over the wrists.
It ended in reverse fashion:
pouring water over the wrists,
then the fingers, then the fingertips.
Jesus did not disdain such rituals.
He disdained giving more importance
to them than to God's instruction
to feed the hungry, house the homeless,
and clothe the naked (ISAIAH 58:7).

To what extent does my faith-practice
boil down, mainly, to going to church
and keeping certain regulations?

*When people hear us speak God's word,
they marvel at its beauty and power;
when they see what little impact it has
on our daily lives,
they laugh and poke fun at what we say.*

ANONYMOUS SECOND-CENTURY CHRISTIAN

WEDNESDAY
Ordinary Time
Week 28 _____

[Jesus rebuked some Pharisees, saying,]
"You neglect justice and love for God. . . .
You love the reserved seats
in the synagogues. . . .
How terrible for you!" LUKE 11:42-44

A woman had a strange dream.
An angel took her to a church to worship.
The organist played,
the organ's keys went up and down,
but no music came from the organ.
The choir sang,
the singers' mouths opened and closed,
but no song came from their lips.
The congregation prayed,
their lips moved,
but no sound could be heard.
The woman turned to the angel and said,
"Why don't I hear anything?"
The angel said, "There's nothing to hear."

How faithfully
do I try to worship my God and savior,
not only with my lips
but also with my heart and my life?

In the nineteenth century
the problem was that God is dead;
in the twentieth century
the problem is that man is dead.
ERICH FROMM

*[One day Jesus confronted some teachers
with the "Wisdom of God,"
which says,] " 'I will send them
prophets and messengers;
they will kill some of them
and persecute others.' "*

LUKE 11:49

In his book *The Brothers Karamazov,*
Feodor Dostoevski notes that people
reject their prophets and slay them.
Then they turn around and
"honor those whom they have slain."
Many religious leaders in Jesus' time
found themselves in a similar situation.
They honored the prophets
their fathers had killed (LUKE 11:48),
while they themselves killed prophets,
like John the Baptist and Jesus.
The irony continues to our own day.
Martin Luther King, Jr., was persecuted
and killed by some of the fathers
whose sons now honor him.

Why do I find it hard, sometimes,
to accept contemporary prophets?
Who might one of these prophets be?

*Let us not look back in anger,
nor forward in fear,
but around in awareness.*
JAMES THURBER

FRIDAY
Ordinary Time
Week 28 _____

*[Jesus said,] "Not one sparrow
is forgotten by God. . . .
So do not be afraid; you are worth
much more than many sparrows!"*

LUKE 12:6-7

A young woman was unchurched
for 12 years, having left in college.
She and her husband had just moved.
Since both were avid readers,
there were literally dozens of boxes
of books stacked up, still unpacked.
One night she sat rereading *The Robe,*
in which a Roman soldier becomes
a Christian after watching Jesus die.
She recalled *Mere Christianity,*
a book she had been given years ago.
She felt strangely moved to read it now.
It turned out to be the first book
in the first box she opened,
and it contained exactly what she needed.
The next day she returned to Church.

When did I sense God's hand guiding me
at a critical moment in my life—
when I had, perhaps, forgotten God?

*I will never forget you. . . .
I have written your name
on the palms of my hands.*

ISAIAH 49:15-16

*[Jesus said,] "Whoever declares publicly
that he [or she] belongs to me,
the Son of Man will do the same for him
[or her] before the angels of God."*

LUKE 12:8

In their book *The Conway Twitty Story,*
Cross and Kosser tell how
the country music star felt a bit envious
when other singers shot up ahead of him.
Then one day someone told Conway a story
that took away his envy.
A missionary who had spent his life in China
and a singer who had spent two weeks there
returned home on the same boat.
Thousands met the singer,
but nobody met the missionary.
"Lord," said the missionary, "I gave you
my life and he gave you only 14 days.
Yet thousands welcome him home,
and nobody welcomes me home."
The Lord replied,
"My son, you're not home yet."

To what extent do I seek or expect
recognition for what I do in this world?

*[Jesus said,] "Store up riches . . .
in heaven. . . . For your heart will
always be where your riches are."*

MATTHEW 6:20-21

SUNDAY
Ordinary Time
Week 29 _____

*[Some Pharisees tried to trap Jesus
by asking him if it was lawful
to pay taxes to the emperor.
Jesus foiled their plot to involve him
in a political controversy, saying,]*
*"Repay to Caesar what belongs to Caesar
and to God what belongs to God."*

MATTHEW 22:21 (NAB)

Many professional beekeepers
tend their beehives without putting on
special veils or clothing.
How do they avoid being stung?
Their technique is simple.
They remain perfectly calm
and move about slowly and deliberately.
This keeps the bees calm and cool.
Thus, even when scores of bees
land on a keeper's unprotected skin,
the keeper does not yield to panic.
Jesus also mastered the virtue
of staying calm in heated situations.
We see him do that in today's reading.

To what extent
do I try to remain cool and in control
when others attack me—even unfairly?

*Anger is the wind
that blows out the lamp of the mind.*

ROBERT INGERSOLL

[Jesus told this parable.
"A farmer decided to tear down his barns
and build bigger ones to store his riches.
That night he died, leaving all behind."]
Jesus concluded,
"This is how it is with those
who pile up riches for themselves
but are not rich in God's sight."

LUKE 12:21

Murray Garsson and his brother owned
a $75 million business during World War II.
Ten years later, the *Detroit Free Press*
carried this brief report:
"Garsson, penniless and homeless,
died last night in Belleview Hospital,
where he was taken
after he had been sleeping for three weeks
in his physician's waiting room . . .
because he was broke."

Jesus' parable and Garsson's story
invite me to inventory my own life.
Is the focus of my priorities
more on *acquiring* or more on *becoming*?
What is, perhaps, the best indication
of where my focus lies?

I can't get too excited about anything
that won't fit in my coffin.

COMEDIAN FRED ALLEN

TUESDAY
Ordinary Time
Week 29 —————————————

[About the Son of Man's return,
Jesus said,] "How happy they are
if he finds them ready,
even if he should come
at midnight or even later!"

LUKE 12:38

James Matthew Barrie has enriched
our world with such plays as
The Admirable Crichton and *Peter Pan.*
We don't know if Barrie had a list
of favorite Scripture passages.
But if he did, we might find
today's reading among them.
For Barrie once said
that the most dangerous day in our lives
is when we discover the word *tomorrow.*
On that day we learn to procrastinate.

Today's reading talks about
being ready for Jesus' second coming.
In a wider sense, however,
it talks about being ready for
that equally unknown hour
when death will come for us.
How ready am I for that hour?

Lord, when death comes,
may I be able to say what Jesus said:
["Father,] I have finished the work
you gave me to do."   JOHN 17:4

WEDNESDAY
Ordinary Time
Week 29

*[Jesus said,] "Much is required
from the person to whom much is given;
much more is required from the person
to whom much more is given."*

LUKE 12:48

In his book *Through Seasons of the Heart*,
John Powell writes:
"God sends each person into this world
with a special message to deliver,
with a special song to sing . . .
with a special act of love to bestow."

This raises a question:
How do I discover what my special song,
message, or act of love is?

*God has committed some work to me
which he has not committed to another.
I have my mission—
I may never know it in this life,
but I shall be told it in the next. . . .
[Therefore] I can never be thrown away.
If I am in sickness,
my sickness may serve him;
if I am in sorrow,
my sorrow may serve him. . . .
[God] does nothing in vain. . . .
O my God, I put myself
without reserve into your hands.*

JOHN HENRY NEWMAN

368

[Jesus said,]
"I came to set the earth on fire,
and how I wish
it were already kindled! . . .
Do you suppose that I came
to bring peace to the world?
No, not peace, but division."

LUKE 12:49, 51

Frank Shallard
is a fundamentalist preacher
in Sinclair Lewis's novel *Elmer Gantry*.
As he grows old, he also grows cynical.
One day he asks a friend,
"Just what are the teachings of Christ?
Did he come to bring peace or more war?
He says both."
Shallard's question is like asking,
Do stairs go up or do they go down?
Jesus' teaching is something like that.
It brings peace to those who seek truth,
fire to those who seek something else.

What might I do when someone I love
rejects Jesus' teaching
because he or she is closed to truth?

Lord, may your fire bring
light where there is darkness and
warmth where there is coldness.
May it purify me, and not destroy me.

FRIDAY
Ordinary Time
Week 29

*[Jesus said,] "When you see a cloud
coming up in the west, at once you say that
it is going to rain—and it does. . . .
You can look at the earth and the sky
and predict the weather;
why, then, don't you know the meaning
of this present time?"*   LUKE 12:54, 56

Paul Brodeur calls statistics
"human beings with tears wiped off."
His description is especially fitting
when it comes to alcohol.
Seventy traffic deaths a day
are alcohol related.
Seventy percent of all drownings and
eighty percent of all fire fatalities
are alcohol related.
Finally, the cost to our national economy
in lost production due to alcohol
is almost $50 billion annually.
Similar statistics could be compiled
for drugs and smoking.

In light of Jesus' question at the end
of today's reading, what meaning
might I attach to the above statistics?
What is one thing I might do about them?

Problems loom large when men don't.
            ROBERT J. BIDINOTTO

SATURDAY
Ordinary Time
Week 29 _____

[Jesus said to a group of Galileans,]
"I tell you
that if you do not turn from your sins,
you will all die." LUKE 13:3

A thief stole a tape recorder
from a church in Florida.
Later, when he got it home,
he saw that there was a tape
in the machine.
Curious to know what was on the tape,
the thief pressed the Play button
and listened.
It was a sermon by the pastor,
inviting his listeners
to heed these words of Jesus:
"Turn from your sins."
The thief was so moved by what he heard
that he returned the tape recorder
and reformed his life.

If Jesus appeared right now before me,
and asked lovingly,
"What is one evil tendency
that you would like me to heal you of?"
what would I say?

There is actually
one thing worse than evil itself,
and that is indifference to evil.
JOSEPH FLETCHER

SUNDAY
Ordinary Time
Week 30

[Jesus said,]
" 'Love your neighbor as . . . yourself.' "
MATTHEW 22:39

A TV documentary, "The Civil War,"
took audiences by storm in 1990.
One program in the eleven-part series
featured a letter written by Sullivan Ballou
to his wife, Sarah,
just before the first battle of Bull Run.
Realizing he might be killed, he wrote:
"How hard it is to . . . burn to ashes
the hopes of future years when,
God willing, we might still have lived
and loved together to see our boys
grown to honorable manhood around us.
If I do not return, my dear Sarah,
never forget how much I loved you,
nor that when my last breath
escapes me on the battlefield,
it will whisper your name. Forgive . . .
the many pains I have caused you.
How thoughtless . . . I have sometimes been."
Sullivan was killed at Bull Run.

How readily do I express my feelings
to my loved ones?

*I shall always be with you in the
brightest day and in the darkest night.*
SULLIVAN BALLOU to Sarah

MONDAY
Ordinary Time
Week 30 —————————————

[A woman] was bent over
and could not straighten up at all.
When Jesus saw her,
he called out . . . ,
"Woman, you are free . . . !"
He placed his hands on her,
and at once she straightened herself up
and praised God.   LUKE 13:11-13

Dr. Norman Lobsenz wrote an article
entitled "The Loving Message of Touch."
It cites several studies to show that *touch*
plays a big role in people's lives.
For example,
children who enjoy a high degree
of physical contact with parents
are far healthier than those who do not.
They have higher IQs,
walk sooner, and talk sooner.
Reading the studies, you wonder,
"If ordinary human touch has such power,
think of the power
that the touch of Jesus must have had.

How do I use the gift of touch?

But, O, for the touch
of a vanish'd hand,
And the sound of
a voice that is still!
ALFRED, LORD TENNYSON

Jesus asked,
"What is the Kingdom of God like?
What shall I compare it with?
It is like this.
A man takes a mustard seed
and plants it. . . .
The plant grows and becomes a tree."

LUKE 13:18-19

Some young Christians were attending
an international summer camp.
One project the leaders assigned them
was to think up more effective ways
to spread God's word in the world.
The most provocative suggestion
came from an African girl, who said:
"When Christians in my country
think a pagan village
is ready for Christianity,
they don't send books or missionaries.
They send a good Christian family.
The example of the family
converts the village."

Why would/wouldn't your family
qualify for such a mission?

Not the cry,
but the flight of the wild duck
leads the flock to fly and follow.
CHINESE PROVERB

WEDNESDAY
Ordinary Time
Week 30 _____

*[Jesus told the people,] "Do your best
to go in through the narrow door
[that leads to God's Kingdom]; . . .
many people will surely try . . .
but will not be able."*   LUKE 13:24

A *Peanuts* cartoon shows Charlie Brown
in his house, staring at the front door.
He wants to go outside to ski, but is
too bundled up to pass through the door.
Finally, he shouts, "Well, how am I
supposed to get through the door?"
Charlie's frustration is one
that many modern Christians have.
They want to pass through the door
that leads to God's Kingdom.
But they are too "bundled up"
in the "good things" of this life to do it.
So, like Charlie,
they stand in front of it and shout,
"Well, how am I
supposed to get through the door?"

If my house were burning down
and I could rescue only one thing—
money excluded—what would I select?

*When we begin to live more seriously inside,
we begin to live more simply outside.*
ERNEST HEMINGWAY

[Jesus said,]
"Jerusalem, Jerusalem! . . .
How many times I wanted
to put my arms around all your people,
just as a hen gathers her chicks
under her wings,
but you would not let me!" LUKE 13:34

A speaker was giving a talk to parents.
He stressed the need to reach out more
to children, especially teenagers.
After he had finished,
a mother said,
"You've talked a lot about our failure
to reach out to our children.
I've reached out again and again
to my teenage son,
but he rejects my efforts—
often coldly and cruelly.
Tell me what I'm supposed to do now."
Jesus knew how that mother felt.
He, too, experienced cruel rejection.

How do I respond
when my overtures of love
are rejected coldly—and even cruelly?

No one needs love more
than someone who doesn't deserve it.
AUTHOR UNKNOWN

FRIDAY
Ordinary Time
Week 30 _____

[A man in need of healing
came to Jesus on the Sabbath.]
Jesus took the man, healed him,
and sent him away.
Then he said to [those present
who opposed healing on the Sabbath],
"If any one of you had a son or an ox
that happened to fall in a well
on a Sabbath, would you not
pull him out at once?" LUKE 14:2, 5

Humorist Will Rogers had the ability
to get right to the heart of things.
Jesus had a similar ability.
For example, he said to some Pharisees,
who said it was against Jewish law
to heal people on the Sabbath:
" 'What does our Law
allow us to do on the Sabbath?
To help or to harm?
To save a man's life or to destroy it?'
But they did not say a thing" (MARK 3:4).

To what extent is it true
that love does not do away with law,
but that law can do away with love?

The worse sin is not to hate people
but to be coldly indifferent to them.
GEORGE BERNARD SHAW (slightly adapted)

[Jesus said,]
"Everyone who makes himself great
will be humbled,
and everyone who humbles himself
will be made great."   LUKE 14:11

One of Pope John XXIII's first acts
as pope was to visit Regina Coeli,
a large prison in Rome.
The pope confided to the inmates
that his cousin had served time.
The official Vatican newspaper,
L'Osservatore Romano,
thought its readers might be shocked
to learn that a papal relative
had been in prison.
So it omitted this remark
in reporting the pope's visit to prison.
During the next four years,
the humble pope
kept the newspaper's editor busy
editing out papal "indiscretions."

Do I tend to exalt or to humble myself?

You may fool those who work above you;
you may fool those who work around you;
but you will rarely fool those
who work under you.

ANONYMOUS

SUNDAY
Ordinary Time
Week 31 _____

*[Jesus rebuked the Pharisees
and the scribes, saying,]
"They don't practice what they preach. . . .
They do everything so that people
will see them."*   MATTHEW 23:3, 5

An army major was in his new office
when a private appeared at the door.
To impress the private, the major said,
"Come in, soldier! Be right with you
after I answer this phone call."
Then speaking into the phone, he said,
"Well, General, good to hear your voice.
How can I help you?" A pause followed.
Then the major said, "Fine, General,
I'll call the President within the hour!"
Then he said to the private,
who was staring at the floor nervously,
"Now, soldier, what can I do for you?"
Without looking up,
the private said in a low voice,
"The sergeant told me to come in
and hook up your telephone for you."

When was the last time
I tried to impress another in some way?
How prevalent is this in my life?

*Character is much easier kept
than recovered.*

THOMAS PAINE

[Jesus said,]
"When you give a feast, invite the poor,
the crippled, the lame, and the blind;
and you will be blessed, because
they are not able to pay you back.
God will repay you on the day
the good people rise from death."

LUKE 14:13-14

A businessman met with the president
of a private Chicago high school.
To show his appreciation
for what the school had done
for his sons, he had decided to set up
a scholarship for needy students.
After working out all the details,
the president said to the businessman,
"Would you give us the honor of letting
the scholarship bear your name?"
The businessman said, "Let it bear
any name you wish, except mine.
I didn't give it for that reason."

When was the last time
I made some contribution or
performed some service,
requesting to remain anonymous?

Character, like a photograph,
develops in darkness.

YOUSSUF KARSH

TUESDAY
Ordinary Time
Week 31 _____

*[Jesus told this parable about a master
who invited guests to a feast.]*
*"But they all began, one after another,
to make excuses. . . . The master was furious
and said to his servant,
'Hurry out to the streets and alleys
of the town, and bring back the poor,
the crippled, the blind, and the lame . . .
so that my house may be full.' "*

LUKE 14:18, 21, 23

A retired person says,
"I want to volunteer my service
to help the needy, but I'm not ready yet."
A college student says,
"I want to tutor slower students,
but I don't think I'd be any good at it."
Both of these people
are modern examples of the people
Jesus talks about in his parable.
They are "excuse people."

What is one thing I've considered doing
but keep putting off?
What is one good reason
for not checking into it today?

*The impersonal hand of government
can never replace
the helping hand of a neighbor.*

HUBERT H. HUMPHREY

WEDNESDAY
Ordinary Time
Week 31

Once when large crowds of people
were going along with Jesus,
he turned and said to them . . .
"Whoever does not carry his own cross
and come after me
cannot be my disciple."

LUKE 14:25, 27

"The Muckers" is a poem by Carl Sandburg.
Set in the depression years,
it describes workers digging a ditch.
The job is dirty and dangerous.
Some workers wallow knee-deep in mud.
Above the ditch are unemployed workers,
watching the diggers.
Half of the watchers say to themselves,
"What a tough job to have."
The others say, "I wish I had that job."
Sandburg's point is this:
It is painful to work;
but it is also painful to be without work.
Today's reading makes a similar point
about discipleship.
It is painful to be a disciple,
but it is also painful not to be one.

How grateful am I for my discipleship?
How generously do I live it out?

The cost of being a disciple is big;
the cost of not being one is bigger still.

THURSDAY
Ordinary Time
Week 31 _____

[Jesus gave this example. "Suppose you
had a hundred sheep and lost one.
What would you do? You'd leave the other
ninety-nine and look for the lost one.
When you found it, you'd be overjoyed."
Jesus concluded,] "In the same way . . .
there will be more joy in heaven
over one sinner who repents
than over ninety-nine respectable people
who do not need to repent." LUKE 15:7

A teacher asked her students to update
Jesus' Parable of the Lost Sheep.
One student wrote: "Suppose you
finish typing a 100-page term paper.
Then you discover one sheet is missing.
What do you do? You search for it.
When you find it, you are so happy
that you throw the other 99 sheets
into the air, saying,
'Yippee! I found my lost sheet!'
That's how God feels
when you start back to church again."

Have I tried to help an inactive Christian
become active again? How?

Problems are only opportunities
with thorns on them.
HUGH MILLER

*[Jesus told a parable about a manager
who was caught wasting money.
Before being terminated, he cancelled
parts of debts that people owed his boss.
Thus, he won friends who would help him
after his dismissal. Jesus said of him,]*
*"The people of this world are much more
shrewd in handling their affairs
than the people who belong to the light."*

LUKE 16:8

A mother had just kissed her son,
who was leaving for camp.
She said to an older mother next to her,
"A month is a long time
not to hear from a seven-year-old.
I wish I knew how to get him to write."
"It's simple," said the older mother.
"When you send him a letter, say,
'Enclosed is five dollars.'"
The younger mother said, "That works?"
"Like a charm," said the older mother.
"He'll write instantly, saying,
'You forgot to enclose the five dollars.'"

Am I more resourceful and diligent
in handling the affairs of this short life
than the never-ending life to come?

Life is the flash of a firefly in the night.
CROWFOOT

SATURDAY
Ordinary Time
Week 31 _____

[Jesus said,]
"The things that are considered
of great value by man
are worth nothing in God's sight."
LUKE 16:15

Jerry Kramer was a pro football star.
Near the end of his career, he wrote
a best-seller called *Instant Replay:*
The Green Bay Diary of Jerry Kramer.
One passage reads:
"I remember reading John O'Hara's
The Last Laugh about a movie star
who had been an SOB all his life
and at the end of the book
after he had gone completely downhill,
he said something like this:
'At least I've been a big-time movie star
and nobody can take that away from me.' "
Kramer comments, "Big deal. Who cares?"

What is one thing
that I valued highly at one time in life
but no longer value as highly? Why?

Life is not lost by dying!
Life is lost minute by minute,
day by dragging day,
in all the thousand, small,
uncaring ways.
STEPHEN VINCENT BENET

*[Jesus told a parable to warn us
to stay alert for his second coming.
Ten bridesmaids were at a bride's house
to welcome the groom.
Night fell, and he didn't arrive. Result?
The maids dozed off and five of them
missed his arrival.] Jesus concluded,
"Watch out, then,
because you do not know the day
or the hour [of the Son of Man's coming]."*

MATTHEW 25:13

Swiss psychiatrist Dr. Paul Tournier
dates his conversion to a day
when he chose to spend an hour praying.
It proved to be a dry, painful experience.
But when the hour was over,
something told him to pray a bit longer.
He did and ended up
experiencing God's presence in a way
that changed his life.
It frightened him to think
how close he had come to missing it.

Do I sometimes tend to shorten or prolong
my period of prayer
when it is a dry, painful experience?

*It is better to be patient than powerful.
It is better to win control over yourself
than over whole cities.* PROVERBS 16:32

MONDAY
Ordinary Time
Week 32 _____

Jesus said to his disciples,
"Things that make people fall into sin
are bound to happen,
but how terrible for the one
who makes them happen!"   LUKE 17:1

An old man lay dying.
Something was clearly troubling him.
Finally, he broke the silence, saying:
"When I was a boy,
I used to play in a field
near the intersection of two roads.
There was an old signpost there,
and I used to twist it so that the arrows
pointed unsuspecting travelers
down the wrong roads.
As I lie here now,
I wonder how many people
I misdirected or hurt by doing that—
and other sinful acts."

Jesus' words and the dying man's story
invite me to ask myself:
What is one way, right now,
that I could be misdirecting others?

When I was young,
I admired clever people.
Now that I am old, I admire kind people.
                    ABRAHAM HESCHEL

*[Jesus said,] "The servant does not deserve
thanks for obeying orders. . . .
It is the same with you;
when you have done
all you have been told to do, say,
'We . . . have only done our duty.'"*

LUKE 17:9-10

TV Guide carried a candid article
about an actor's evaluation
of his performance in a TV series. He said,
"I've given the show a real shortchange.
I don't feel I've given it 25 percent."
When asked if he shortchanged it
because he disliked it, the actor said,
"No, I was just lazy."
We can relate to the actor's comment.
We've all shortchanged responsibilities:
duties, jobs, relationships.
Touching on this point someone said,
"It's gotten to the point
where I expect a reward or a bonus
for doing things
that I ought to have done anyway."

On a scale of one (low) to ten (high),
how would I rate my performance
as a family person? As a Christian?

Work is love made visible.
KAHLIL GIBRAN

WEDNESDAY
Ordinary Time
Week 32

[One day a group of lepers cried out,]
"Jesus! Master! Have pity on us!"
Jesus . . . said to them,
"Go and let the priests examine you."
On the way they were made clean.
[But only one returned to give thanks.]

LUKE 17:13-14

John Hughes was a taxi driver
in New York City for over 35 years.
One night, while cleaning up his cab,
he found an emerald ring.
He racked his brain to try to recall
to which fare it could have belonged.
Finally, he remembered a woman
with a lot of bundles.
It took him two days to locate her.
Excitedly, he returned the ring.
Not only did the woman
fail to reward him,
but she didn't even thank him.
John said later,
"I was glad I sought her out anyway.
It was what I should have done."

What would have been my response
to the woman's lack of gratitude?

Blessed is he who expects no gratitude,
for he shall not be disappointed.

W. C. BENNETT

THURSDAY
Ordinary Time
Week 32

[Jesus said, "God's Kingdom
doesn't come in a way that can be seen.]
No one will say, 'Look, here it is!'
or, 'There it is!'; because
the Kingdom of God is within you."

LUKE 17:21

A four-year-old girl
was standing with her grandfather
beside an old-fashioned open well.
They had just drawn water to drink.
"Grandfather," the little girl asked,
"where does God live?"
The old man picked her up,
held her over the well, and said,
"Look down and tell me what you see."
Seeing her reflection in the water,
the little girl said, "I see myself."
"Ah!" said her grandfather.
"That's where God lives—in you."
God's Kingdom is like that, too.
It is in the human heart—
where love is.

How deeply do I believe Paul's words,
"You are God's temple" (I CORINTHIANS 3:16)?

Thou who are at home
deep in my heart,
help me to join you deep in my heart.

THE TALMUD

FRIDAY
Ordinary Time
Week 32

*[Speaking of the day when God's Kingdom
will reach its intended completion,
Jesus said, "It will come unexpectedly.]
It will be as it was in the time of Lot.
Everybody kept on eating and drinking . . .
planting and building."*   LUKE 17:28

We might compare
the Kingdom of God to a child.
A child is very much alive and growing,
but hasn't yet reached adulthood.
The Kingdom of God is like that.
It is very much alive and growing,
but hasn't yet reached maturity.
A question arises.
When will the Kingdom reach maturity?
When can we expect
Jesus to come in final glory
to announce the long-awaited end?
No one knows! This is why Jesus said,
"You also must always be ready"
(MATTHEW 24:44).

How well am I heeding 2 Peter 3:14?
"As you wait for that Day, do your best
to be pure and faultless in God's sight
and to be at peace with him."

We work to become, not to acquire.
                    ELBERT HUBBARD

[Jesus told this parable
to teach people to persevere in prayer.
"A widow kept badgering an unjust judge
for justice. Finally, he relented, saying,]
'Because of all the trouble
this widow is giving me,
I will see to it that she gets her rights.'"

LUKE 18:5

Waiting can be frustrating,
because we're not in control.
Similarly, prayer can be frustrating,
because we're not in control—God is!
This means that our wayward hearts
can sometimes wander during prayer.
What should we do when this happens?
Saint Francis de Sales answers:
"Bring your
wayward heart back home quietly.
Return it tenderly to its Master's side.
If you did nothing else during prayer
but return your heart continually
and patiently to the Master's side,
your prayer time would be well spent."

What is the biggest difficulty
I experience in my daily prayer efforts?

In prayer, the important thing
is not to think much but to love much.

SAINT TERESA OF AVILA

SUNDAY
Ordinary Time
Week 33 _____

*[A master
gave money to some servants to invest.
He praised those who made a profit,
saying,] "You have been faithful
in managing small amounts, so I will
put you in charge of large amounts."*

MATTHEW 25:21

Booker T. Washington
was a black American slave.
At the age of sixteen,
he walked almost five hundred miles
from his slave home
to Hampton Institute in Virginia.
When he got there,
he was told that classes were filled.
Undaunted, he took a job at the school
doing menial jobs:
sweeping floors and making beds.
He did these so well that the faculty
found room for him as a student.
He worked his way up at the school,
became a famed teacher, and eventually
founded Tuskegee Institute in Alabama.

What were some *small* jobs I did well,
before I was given *larger* jobs?

*Do not let what you can't do
interfere with what you can do.*

Basketball coach JOHN WOODEN

MONDAY
Ordinary Time
Week 33

*[A blind man heard
that Jesus was passing by.]
He cried out, "Jesus! Son of David!
Have mercy on me!"* . . .
*Jesus stopped and . . . asked him,
"What do you want me to do for you?"
"Sir," he answered, "I want to see again."*

LUKE 18:38, 40

A teacher read the above passage.
Then she said to her students:
"Imagine you are alone praying.
Jesus appears and asks you,
'What do you want me to do for you?'
What would you say?"
Here are some student responses:
"Give me courage to quit smoking."
"Give me back my childhood faith."
"Take away my depression."
"Give me confidence in myself."

These responses invite me to ask:
What would I ask for
if Jesus appeared to me and asked,
"What do you want me to do for you?"

*Prayer is an expression of who we are. . . .
We are a living incompleteness.
We are a gap, an emptiness
that calls for fulfillment.*

THOMAS MERTON

TUESDAY
Ordinary Time
Week 33 _____

[Zacchaeus wanted to see Jesus.
But the crowd was big and he was short.
So he ran ahead, climbed a tree,
and waited.
Jesus saw him and said,]
"Hurry down, Zacchaeus,
because I must stay in your house today."
Zacchaeus hurried down. . . .
The people . . . started grumbling,
"This man has gone as a guest
to the home of a sinner!"   LUKE 19:5-7

It was the day of the 1984 playoffs
between the Cubs and the Padres
at Chicago's Wrigley Field.
The TV camera zoomed in on fans
on rooftops and on light poles.
One humorous shot showed a fan
in a tree just beyond the left-field wall.
It recalled the story in today's gospel.

The stories of the two tree climbers
make an important point:
Where there's a will, there's a way.
They also make me ask myself:
How badly do I want to see Jesus?
What tree am I ready to climb for him?

Discipline is remembering what you want.
                              DAVID CAMPBELL

WEDNESDAY
Ordinary Time
Week 33

*["A merchant was leaving on a long trip.
Before going, he called his ten servants
and gave each a gold coin to invest
during his absence.
Upon his return,] he ordered his servants
to appear before him, in order to find out
how much they had earned.
[He rewarded them according to how well
each had invested the gold coin."]*

LUKE 19:15

Years ago, most daily papers carried
"Believe It or Not."
It dealt with incredible facts.
For example, one of the features
showed an iron bar worth $5.
The feature went on to say
that the same iron bar could be made
into horseshoes worth $50,
into needles worth $5,000, or
into watch springs worth $500,000.

This recalls today's gospel story.
It invites me to ask: What am I making
with my God-given talents?

*Having only modest talent
is no excuse for not using it.
Think what the morning would be like
if only talented birds sang!*

ANONYMOUS

THURSDAY
Ordinary Time
Week 33 _____

[Jesus wept over Jerusalem, saying,]
"They will completely destroy you
and . . . not a single stone
will they leave in its place,
because you did not recognize the time
when God came to save you!"

LUKE 19:44

In his play *Julius Caesar,*
Shakespeare reflects upon the tragedy
of missed opportunities. He writes:
"There is a tide in the affairs of men
Which, taken at the flood,
leads on to fortune;
Omitted, all the voyage of life
Is bound in shallows and in miseries."
This happened
to Jerusalem and its people.
They did not heed Jesus' call to repent.
They let salvation slip like sand
through their fingers.
True to Jesus' words in today's gospel,
Roman armies leveled Jerusalem
in A.D. 70.

Can I recall a time in my life
when God gave me a special opportunity
to grow spiritually?

Conscience is God's presence within us.
EMMANUEL SWEDENBORG

[Jesus drove sellers out of the Temple, saying,] "It is written in the Scriptures that God said, 'My Temple will be called a house of prayer.' But you have turned it into a hideout for thieves!" LUKE 19:46

The Temple had four courts:
four special areas of worship
for priests, men, women, and Gentiles.
Sacrificial animals and doves were sold
quietly in the court of the Gentiles.
But soon the quiet atmosphere
of the court of the Gentiles
degenerated into a noisy market.
Worse yet, unscrupulous sellers
began exploiting unsuspecting pilgrims.
When Temple authorities didn't step in,
Jesus did.

Jesus' concern for
an atmosphere of prayer in the Temple
recalls the enriching role
that atmosphere plays in prayer.
It invites me to consider if a candle,
a crucifix, or a statue might provide
a richer atmosphere for my own prayer.

*When beauty overwhelms us . . .
we are close to worship.*

RICHARD C. CABOT

SATURDAY
Ordinary Time
Week 33 _____

[Some Sadducees questioned
Jesus' teaching about life after death.
Jesus responded,] "Moses clearly proves
that the dead are raised to life. . . .
He speaks of the Lord as
'the God of Abraham, the God of Isaac,
and the God of Jacob.'
He is the God of the living,
not of the dead, for to him all are alive."

LUKE 20:37–38

A soldier was in a trench with his buddy.
Suddenly a shell exploded yards away.
Miraculously he lived, but his buddy died.
The soldier wrote: "The corpse lying
on the ground was not my friend.
It was only an empty shell,
close to nothing at all.
My friend's intellect, his knowledge,
his spirit, his charm—all of these
had departed the shell on the ground.
It was then that I *knew*
that something we call the 'soul'
survives the body after death."

How deep is my faith in life after death?

Our Lord has written the promise
of the resurrection not in books alone,
but in every leaf in springtime.

MARTIN LUTHER

SUNDAY
Ordinary Time
Week 34

[At the Last Judgment the King will say,]
" 'I was a stranger and you received me. . . .'
The righteous will then answer . . .
'When, Lord, did we . . . welcome you . . . ?'
The King will reply,
'I tell you, whenever you did this
for one of the least important . . .
you did it for me!' "　　　　　MATTHEW 25:35, 37-38, 40

Two young people were canoeing
in the Canadian wilds and were weary.
Suddenly they spotted a trapper's cabin.
It was unlocked and clean.
In it was an open Bible, with this note:
"Your cabin saved my life.
I was seriously ill and needed shelter.
Your cabin provided it. I can't repay you
with money, only with God's blessing.
Read Matthew 25:31ff" (today's reading).
Later, one of the young people said,
"I'd read that passage often,
but I never understood it until that day."

Since starting this program,
what one gospel passage
has struck me in a special way?

Lay hold of the Bible
until the Bible lays hold of you.
WILLIAM H. HOUGHTON

MONDAY
Ordinary Time
Week 34 _____

*[A widow put into the offering box
"two little copper coins." Jesus said,]
"This poor widow put in more
than all the others.
For the others offered their gifts
from what they had to spare . . .
but she . . . gave all she had to live on."*

LUKE 21:3-4

In *How to Be a Winning Loser,*
Jim Macholtz rewrites today's gospel
for young athletes.
His rewrite goes something like this:
"A high school coach and his assistants
were watching the track team work out.
After the team had gone through
a particularly tough exercise,
the coach pointed to a runner
who had little natural ability and said,
'That kid put forth
more effort than all the others.
The others dug deep,
but he gave everything he had.
He had absolutely nothing left to give.' "

On a scale of one (little) to ten (great),
how much effort am I putting forth
in my spiritual race for eternal life?

Don't bunt. Aim out of the ballpark.
DAVID OGILVY

TUESDAY
Ordinary Time
Week 34

[One day Jesus warned his disciples
about the end times, saying,]
"Watch out; don't be fooled.
Many men, claiming to speak for me,
will come and say, 'I am he!'
and, 'The time has come!'
But don't follow them."   LUKE 21:8

The movie *Firstborn* deals with
a mother and her two young sons.
She has been abandoned by her husband
and has lived a lonely life for two years.
Then a man moves in with her.
The boys mistrust him instantly and
try to warn their mother, but to no avail.
Finally, the boys' fears materialize,
and they barely escape with their lives.
It is so easy
to misread people and situations.
This is Jesus' point in today's reading:
"Watch out; don't be fooled," he warns.
"Many men, claiming to speak for me,
will come. . . . But don't follow them."

How might Jesus' warning be relevant
for my spiritual life right now?

A famous recipe for rabbit stew begins,
"Catch rabbit!"
Sometimes we overlook the obvious.

WEDNESDAY
Ordinary Time
Week 34 _____

[Jesus warned his disciples
about the end times, saying,]
"Everyone will hate you because of me.
But not a single hair from your heads
will be lost. Stand firm,
and you will save yourselves."

LUKE 21:17-19

England's future looked bleak in 1939.
Hitler's armies appeared invincible.
King George VI addressed his people
and counseled them to trust God.
He ended by quoting from the poem
"God Knows," by Minnie Louise Haskins:
"I said to the man
who stood at the gate of the year,
'Give me a light that I may tread safely
into the unknown!'
And he replied: 'Go out into the darkness
and put your hand into the hand of God.
That shall be to you better than light
and safer than a known way.'"
The king's counsel to his people echoes
Jesus' counsel to his disciples: trust God.

How much trust do I have in God's
love and concern for me personally?

Some things
have to be believed to be seen.

RALPH HODGSON

*[Jesus said,] "People will faint from fear
as they wait for what is coming over
the whole earth, for the powers in space
will be driven from their courses.
Then the Son of Man will appear, coming
in a cloud with great power and glory.
When these things begin to happen,
stand up and raise your heads,
because your salvation is near."*

LUKE 21:26-28

The TV movie *The Day After*
was filmed in Lawrence, Kansas, in 1983.
It dealt with what that city would be like
the day after a nuclear attack.
Over 100 million viewers watched it.
Newsweek magazine wrote:
"From the boardrooms of Manhattan
to the schoolrooms of San Francisco,
it was one of the most talked about
TV programs in history."
Today's gospel reading reads like
an excerpt from *The Day After.*
There is one big difference.
Jesus tells his disciples not to fear.

What is the greatest fear I have
when it comes to our modern world?

If God is for us, who can be against us?

ROMANS 8:31

FRIDAY
Ordinary Time
Week 34 _____

[Jesus said,] "Think of the . . . trees.
When you see their leaves
beginning to appear,
you know that summer is near.
In the same way, when you see
these things happening, you will know
that the Kingdom of God is about to come."

LUKE 21:29-31

Ancient Greeks believed
that history follows a cyclical pattern.
In other words, every 3,000 years or so
some disaster wipes out the world.
After the disaster, human history
begins all over again, repeating itself.
Christians hold just the opposite.
They believe
that history follows a linear pattern.
In other words, it has definite direction.
Human history is moving
toward the completion of God's Kingdom,
which Jesus set in motion
but left for us to complete.

What am I doing—or trying to do—
to work toward the completion
of God's Kingdom?

There is no such thing as darkness;
only a failure to see.

MALCOLM MUGGERIDGE

*[Jesus warned his disciples about
the end times: "Don't] become occupied
with too much feasting. . . .
Be on watch and pray always
that you will have the strength
to go safely through all those things . . .
and to stand before the Son of Man."*

LUKE 21:34, 36

The *Titanic* sank in 1912,
drowning more than 1,500 people.
Decades later, a magazine asked:
"If you had been on the *Titanic*
when it was sinking,
would you have occupied yourself
rearranging the deck chairs?"
The question seems idiotic at first.
Upon reflection, however,
we see that it makes the same point
that Jesus does in today's gospel reading:
"[Don't] become occupied
with too much feasting. . . .
Be on watch and pray always
that you will have the strength
to go safely through all those things."

To what extent am I "rearranging
the deck chairs" on a ship that is sinking?

Trust in God—but tie your camel tight.
PERSIAN PROVERB

YEAR-CYCL

The following table shows w
follow in the upcoming years.

Liturgical Year	Cycle to Follow
1992/93	A
1993/94	B
1994/95	C
1995/96	A
1996/97	B
1997/98	C
1998/99	A
1999/2000	B
2000/1	C
2001/2	A
2002/3	B
2003/4	C
2004/5	A
2005/6	B
2006/7	C
2007/8	A
2008/9	B
2009/10	C

The following table shows which cycle to follow in the upcoming years.

Liturgical Year	Cycle to Follow
1992/93	A
1993/94	B
1994/95	C
1995/96	A
1996/97	B
1997/98	C
1998/99	A
1999/2000	B
2000/1	C
2001/2	A
2002/3	B
2003/4	C
2004/5	A
2005/6	B
2006/7	C
2007/8	A
2008/9	B
2009/10	C

Weekly Meeting Format

CALL TO PRAYER

> *The leader begins each weekly meeting*
> *by having someone light a candle*
> *and then reading the following prayerfully:*

Jesus said,
"I am the light of the world. . . .
Whoever follows me
will have the light of life
and will never walk in darkness."

JOHN 8:12

Lord Jesus, you also said
that where two or three
come together in your name,
you are there with them.
The light of this candle
symbolizes your presence among us.

And, Lord Jesus,
where you are,
there, too,
are the Father and the Holy Spirit.
So we begin our meeting
in the presence and the name
of the Father,
the Son,
and the Holy Spirit.